EVERYDAY
SPEAKING
FOR ALL
OCCASIONS

ALSO BY ELAINE T. PARTNOW

BOOKS

The Female Dramatist
The New Quotable Woman
The Quotable Woman: 1800–1981
The Quotable Woman: Eve–1799
Breaking the Age Barrier
Photographic Artists and Innovators, with Turner Browne

PLAYS AND PERFORMANCE WORKS

Hear Us Roar, A Woman's Connection
Hispanic Women Speak
Movers & Shakers: Living History Portraits of Women
A Visit with Emily Dickinson

EVERYDAY SPEAKING FOR ALL OCCASIONS

How to Express Yourself with Confidence and Ease

SUSAN PARTNOW & ELAINE T. PARTNOW

Produced by The Philip Lief Group, Inc.

Doubleday Direct, Inc.
Garden City, New York

Published by GuildAmerica® Books,
an imprint and registered trademark of
Doubleday Direct, Inc., Department GB,
401 Franklin Avenue,
Garden City, New York 11530

Copyright © 1998 by The Philip Lief Group, Inc.
and Elaine Partnow and Susan Partnow
ISBN: 1-56865-709-9
Jacket and Interior Design by Debbie Glasserman
Printed in the United States of America

To our father, Al Partnow,
whose golden voice and superb salesmanship
taught us many valued lessons
and to our mother, Jeanette Bernstein Partnow,
who always encouraged us to take part

Contents

PART ONE: GETTING STARTED

*Achieve confident speaking skills utilizing simple systems
and techniques laid out here for you.*

> You Were Born to Be a Communicator
> All Speaking Is Public Speaking
> Tools and Skills to Guide You
> Update and Become a Lifelong Learner
> A Book for Women
> Overview of *Everyday Speaking for All Occasions*
> Build on Your Own Charisma

*Transform jitters into dynamic energy with these basic
strategies to relax you and heighten your confidence.*

> Welcome the Butterflies
> Control the Body

PART TWO: MAKING THE JOURNEY—ENTERING PUBLIC SPEAKING

Use Interviews to Talk Your Way to Greater Opportunities
Tame the Media

6: PERSUASION, MOTIVATION, AND INSPIRATION **129**
Make sure your approach fulfills your purpose.

Make a Persuasive Argument
Learn What Motivates People
Honor the Moment: Commemorative Speaking

7: PUT YOUR BEST VOICE FORWARD **147**
You weren't born with your voice; coaching techniques can help develop greater strength, authority, and beauty in your vocal image.

Learn the Elements of Vocal Image
Start with the Breath
Manage Pitch, Volume, and Pacing to Get and Keep
    Attention
Turn Up the Bass
Increase Your Stamina

PART THREE: FINISHING TOUCHES AND ACCESSORIES

8: STAND AND DELIVER **175**
Meet the challenge of formal presentations by incorporating these basics.

Use Your Natural Talents
Mind Your Manners
Let Your Speech Reflect Your Confidence
Tips for Speaking with Power and Poise

9: A TOOLBOX FOR EVERYDAY SPEAKING   **201**

With planning you can reinforce your message by using visual aids and a range of techniques.

Broadcast on All Channels: Visual, Auditory, Kinesthetic
Vary the Pace
Leaven with Laughter
Create the Ambiance You Want
Mastermind the Program
Make Notes to Keep You on Track
Timing Is Everything
Don't Read a Bedtime Story
Put the Multi in the Media
Be Creative
Smile! You're on Camera

10: MAKING THE JOURNEY   **237**

Congratulations! You've begun a lifelong journey; here are simple ways to foster continuous development and refinement of your speaking skills.

Seek Out Opportunities
Make Speaking an Expanded Conversation
Take the Road to Recovery
Acting Natural Doesn't Just Come Naturally: Practice!
Outward Voice, Inner Journey
Bon Voyage

RESOURCES   **247**

Foreword

When editor Gary Krebs of The Philip Lief Group, with whom I'd worked on other projects, called me in the late summer of 1996 to ask if I would be interested in working on a book for Doubleday Direct addressing women on the subject of speaking, I told him that though I thought it was an excellent subject, I wasn't really the right person for the job. Perhaps I'd like to cowrite it with someone, he suggested. "Who?" I asked. "I could try to find someone," he replied. "Or perhaps you know of someone."

A lightbulb went off. "Someone?" I exclaimed. "I've got the perfect person!" "Who?" he asked. "My sister!"

Not only is she a speech therapist with excellent credentials, but for years Susan has also specialized in conducting workshops and seminars on subjects ranging from conflict resolution and time management to speaking in public. Organizations and corporations throughout the state of Washington have prevailed upon her to educate their staffs. I know her to be a great and inspiring teacher, and with her keen sense of language and lively approach to verbal communications, she seemed perfect for this task.

I am proud to say that I have been proven correct. Susan has done a marvelous job organizing and making comprehensive a complex subject and then writing about it in a style that

I believe will speak to anyone who reads it. From the very start, when together we held brainstorming sessions about the organization of the book—the chapter headings and subheadings—through Susan's many rewrites of each chapter, I have seen the material gather shape and substance.

The small part I played in the making of this book falls right in line with my work as a self-made scholar engrossed in the field of women's history, both past and in the making. I am all too aware of how vital it is that women's voices be heard. In fact, for much of the last two decades, I have dedicated myself to assembling the many voices of women in print. It is my hope that these pages will help you, the reader, be heard.

Elaine T. Partnow
Seattle, Washington
July 1997

Preface and Acknowledgments

When I applied for summer jobs during high school, my mother urged me to put myself out there and just go for it, to reach beyond the familiar. I think she felt frustrated and thwarted by her own shyness and acquiescence to safety and security, so she was determined to provide her daughters with the support she never received. For example, when a potential employer asked whether I knew how to use an electric typewriter, my mother told me to say I'd never seen that particular brand before. She knew I would figure it out easily. The employer didn't need to know I'd never even seen an electric typewriter before in my life! Well, it worked. I got the job.

Here I am, doing the same thing again. Agreeing to write this book was a stretch. When I considered the task before me—compiling years of research and experience—I was worried until I heard my mother whisper in my ear, "You're clever. You'll figure it out. Why not a book?" Still, I felt daunted by the challenge of translating into writing what I have shared successfully for years via the spoken word and visual demonstrations. The tension mounted as I searched for ways to encourage my readers to find *their* own voices in speaking, while I was blocked, by fear and uncertainty, from finding *my* own voice in writing. I felt like eighteenth-century-writer Mary Wortley Montagu, who said, "I sometimes give myself admirable advice, but I am incapable of taking it."

As I drafted Chapter 2—the one on managing nervousness—I vowed to practice using the tools I teach: stop, breathe, relax, and visualize success. Be bold, be yourself, and your message will come through! The methods worked. As I began weaving in the stories of my life, writing from the heart, my joy increased, I found my stride, and what I wrote became a lot more interesting for the reader, I suspect, as well as myself. Click! This is the very message I have to convey about being a good speaker. Our women's way of bringing the personal to the everyday makes it possible to find our voice. Because I followed my own advice and wrote from the heart, in the end, writing this book has left me feeling tremendously empowered.

Over the years I have spoken to dozens of groups and helped thousands of men and women on their learning journeys in my workshops and retreats. Working with them has honed and refined the ideas and approaches you'll find here. The success stories they reported back assure me that you, too, can successfully pursue speaking. I've woven into the book people, friends, and events in my life—all to honor these sources of inspiration, support, and learning. I hope they will enjoy discovering their names and those brief tidbits here and there. Also, in the course of writing, I have come to realize how much of my approach and inspiration is built on the experience and models of other speakers I have heard, books I have read, and workshops I have attended. I gratefully acknowledge countless mentors, those who know me and those who don't.

As with any human endeavor, I could never have completed this book without the insights, encouragement, and additional perspectives of others. Thanks to early readers Claire

Driscoll, Merlin Rainwater, Wendy Dahl, and Raz Mason, who helped me blaze a trail into the woods, and to Jon Dobrer who taught us to "play nicely together" in cyberspace. I am thankful for the early guidance and strong vote of confidence of Gary Krebs and LaVonne Carlson-Finnerty at The Philip Lief Group, from Brigid Mellon at Doubleday Direct, and from our agent, Faith Hamlin. And to those who trekked over every chapter with me, my deep thanks for their guidance and contributions: my supportive and enthused sister, Elaine, of course; my devoted and patient husband, Jim Peckenpaugh; and my wonderful editor, Catherine Peck. I suspect I have been spoiled by Catherine's exceptional care, commitment, and appreciativeness. Whenever I felt lost, I always knew I could find moral support and reset my compass by checking in with friends, including DeeDee Evergreen, Aniko Klein Wolfe, Joyce Mork O'Brien, Kathleen Bander, and Janet Staub DeLong, along with my sisters, Elaine Partnow and Judith Partnow Hyman. Computer mavens Gina Hixx and Mark Wilson were there to help in a lurch. And I hope my children, Tyler and Jessica, will forgive the cranky days and delayed meals. Even Jake, our dear dog, was tried and tested.

To write this book, I gathered all this support and followed Ursula LeGuin's wise lead, "The only thing that makes life possible is permanent, intolerable uncertainty; not knowing what comes next." Whistling a happy tune, I developed a new mantra, "I am terrified *and* courageous" and plunged into the world of writing. You can follow a parallel path to become an effective speaker.

I am hoping to pass along the support, faith, and push given to me by my mother, mentors, students, and friends to you, the reader. While I was preparing the manuscript for this book, I wrote the following message and posted it where I could always see it:

> *I am writing this book*
> *with a loving heart and a clear mind*
> *to bring inspiration, courage, and support*
> *to my sisters.*
> *May I find the patience,*
> *discipline,*
> *wisdom,*
> *and creativity to make it so.*

Dear reader, bring your patience and discipline, take some time to follow the guidance of this book, and you will tap the wisdom and creativity within to offer your voice to the world.

Susan Partnow
Seattle, Washington
July, 1997

Everyday Speaking for All Occasions

Part I

Getting
Started

READY, AIM ... INSPIRE!

Achieve confident speaking skills utilizing simple systems and techniques laid out here for you.

*Whoever has received knowledge
and eloquence in speech from God
should not be silent or secretive
but demonstrate it willingly.*
—MARIE DE FRANCE,
FEMALE TROUBADOUR FROM
THE TWELFTH CENTURY

How do you feel about expressing your knowledge and insights in group situations? Many women say that they have trouble speaking effectively, both in informal situations and at events that require public speaking. They report that when they are required to "think on their feet" or are asked to make public presentations, they avoid and reject opportunities that, in fact, they wish they could accept. Others plunge in but feel less than successful in the end.

Speaking with confidence needn't be a problem for you. Using the tools offered in *Everyday Speaking for All Occasions*, you can learn how to embrace every chance to speak and how to turn everyday speaking into extraordinary opportunities for sharing ideas, for networking, for promoting causes, and for advancing in the workplace. It takes motivation, awareness, information, and a commitment to practice. This book provides support, tools, and encouragement. Are you ready to begin?

YOU WERE BORN TO BE A COMMUNICATOR

The human brain comes preloaded with "software" designed to master language and speaking. With exposure to some instruction and confidence building, each of us can speak out in a powerful voice with a powerful message designed to evoke a powerful response in our listeners. You already possess the skills and style you need for speaking. They are innate.

Think of a time when you talked about a concept you understood thoroughly and believed in passionately while in a comfortable and supportive setting with a responsive listener. Picture yourself—your eyes sparkling, your thoughts flowing, completely absorbed in your message. You were interesting to listen to, effective, and dynamic. You were at your best. My message to you is that those same speaking talents are available to you in every situation.

ALL SPEAKING IS PUBLIC SPEAKING

You may be thinking, "But what has public speaking got to do with me and the speaking I do every day?" All speaking is in fact public speaking, and all public speaking is essentially one-on-one conversation. There is always an audience (the listener) and a speaker (the sender of the message), even when we communicate casually. The good news is that you don't have to become a "speaker" to speak effectively. You just have to be yourself, your best self. As Bette Midler once wrote, "Cherish forever what makes you unique, 'cuz you're really a yawn if it goes!"

Here you will find strategies for all occasions, from small intimate gatherings around the dining table to school-board meetings, church functions, graduation ceremonies, and work-related assemblies. There are approaches for impromptu and formal situations, for short talks and long presentations, for memorials and celebrations. Unlike most books on speaking, which focus on the business world, *Everyday Speaking for All Occasions* is designed to help you *personally*, whether the improvement you seek is purely private or necessary for your career.

Everyone can benefit from coaching and training. Are you inexperienced in speaking? Do you tend to avoid public speaking? Or are you a seasoned speaker looking for ways to polish and rejuvenate your skills? Whatever your current level of expertise, you can cultivate a more powerful and dynamic speaking voice, prepare yourself to convene a panel, master the art of fielding questions, and learn to think on your feet.

TOOLS AND SKILLS TO GUIDE YOU

Fortune brought me training, role models, and support that guided me in becoming an effective, comfortable speaker. My father was a talented salesperson with a golden voice. My school years were filled with opportunities to act in plays, speak at assemblies, and facilitate meetings. My early work experience provided a mentor who helped me learn to present in-service training for co-workers. Most women are not as lucky as I have been. Though we may have extensive instruction in written communication, when it comes to speaking, most of us have little or no formal training. School curricula are so filled with academic subjects that skills having to do with speaking—elocution, debate, and rhetoric—have all but disappeared, which is ironic considering that most of our time is spent in oral communication.

Well, here's your chance to begin to make up for lost time and experience. Leaf through the book casually to get the general idea and glean some inspiration. Then pick it up to study a particular chapter whenever you have a specific need. You will recognize your strengths and learn to build on them, and you will recognize some habits that need changing. Take them one at a time. Every small change will help you become a better speaker. The joy and thrill of speaking is that there is always room to grow, experiment, and improve.

UPDATE AND BECOME A LIFELONG LEARNER

Grow and change we must. Communicating today is more challenging than ever. Society has been conditioned to expect instant information, visual effects, and TV-style packaging (with frequent commercial breaks). Our listeners generally have short attention spans, and they expect entertainment, intensity, and dazzle. Everyone seems in a daze of information overload, so we must hone our messages more clearly and elegantly in order to penetrate.

The degree of sophistication, access to information, and scope of knowledge has also expanded for most people, with the result that audiences feel empowered and demand to be respected and dealt with at the same level as the speaker. Still, in this "high tech," impersonal age, the key to success is often in our ability to counteract it with a personal "high touch." Speaking is the medium through which we can still reach people with our passion, our commitment, and our inspiration.

A BOOK FOR WOMEN

This book was written with a female reader in mind. Though the strategies it presents are largely the same as those I advocate for men, *Everyday Speaking for All Occasions* encourages women to honor the prodigious talents and feminine strengths we can bring to the podium.

Why do women need their own book on effective speaking? How we speak is intimately connected with issues of gender and power. People who perceive themselves to be in power feel comfortable speaking in a manner that is direct, clear, and succinct, without worry about reprisals or fear of giving offense. Those who perceive themselves as dependent—and weaker—must listen more than they speak, accommodating the powerful by paying close attention, agreeing most of the time and, when necessary, disagreeing in the most delicate and indirect way. Such has been the difference between male and female patterns for so long that modern women continue to use patterns conditioned by centuries. All of us possess some masculine traits along with our feminine attributes. Men tend to be more assertive, direct speakers, while women tend to be more passive and indirect. Linguist Robin Lakoff explains, "It is not that women are incapable of direct and forthright communication; rather, we have developed the other type (requiring more finesse and skill) in order to do two impossible things at once: get our needs met, and survive."

Robin Lakoff, along with Deborah Tannen and other contemporary linguists, describes women's style of speaking as relationship-oriented. Women engage in *rapport* talk: We speak to express feelings, to understand, and to offer mutual support. We minimize differences and prefer listening, empathizing, and sharing vulnerabilities because the subtext is always "We're alike; we can connect." It is driven by the need to avoid even the appearance of superiority or competition. Though it is a generalization to say so, apparently most of us just don't like the win/lose game.

Men, on the other hand, have been acculturated to deal with the business of the objective universe. Men engage in *report* talk: They speak to solve problems and establish their relative status in the hierarchy. Their subtext is "I'm different. Notice how unique and special I am so you'll know where we stand in relation to one another." Men's job in speaking has long been to get and keep attention, exchange information, and make an impression. In public settings, discussion serves the purpose of jockeying for status. Conversation often becomes a competition because it is vital to avoid being perceived as weak.

Women at the Podium

These characteristics make the challenge of confident public speaking especially complicated for women. If female conditioning urges us to be likable and to remain part of the group—to avoid seeming superior to others—it can be almost painful for some of us to be in a position that calls attention to ourselves, to stand out, or to show what we know, even if our listeners are all women.

Far from being detrimental to speaking, however, the feminine style can be a tremendous asset. Deborah Tannen, author of *You Just Don't Understand,* describes the contrasting styles of two presenters: The man filled the room with his expansive presence, telling stories as if he were preaching to a crowd in church. The woman brought the room in close and told her stories as if she were sitting in her living room with friends. She was humorous and laughed along with her audience, whereas he remained straight-faced after saying something funny. "The woman's public speaking was successful in a private-speaking sort of way, whereas his was successful in a more public-speaking, oratorical way," writes Tannen. All of the suggestions in this book encourage women to use the best parts of the feminine style in developing their own voices.

The Politics of Talking

Just as we should not assume that being indirect or accommodating is undesirable, neither should we assume that women cannot or should not learn to be more direct. To become effective speakers, we need to recognize the power inherent in each style and to adapt our communication style to individual situations. In other words, when speech patterns that are considered *masculine* are called for to accomplish a goal, then we can use them. When those that are considered *feminine* will best support our cause, then we embrace them as powerful, reasonable, and desirable. By gaining access to both styles, we can take a powerful position in every situation.

A final note: Since *Everyday Speaking* is addressed to women, we have chosen to use the feminine pronoun throughout, even when we are referring to audiences. It does not mean, obviously, that we think women speak only to women, but it is a way of emphasizing that women are the audience for this book.

OVERVIEW OF *EVERYDAY SPEAKING FOR ALL OCCASIONS*

Getting Started

Part One helps you manage your nervousness, the key to "getting ready." Believe it or not, you can learn to accept, welcome, and use those butterflies so that you approach speaking challenges with eagerness and energy. Then you will be ready to enter into those unexpected, impromptu speaking situations. Anticipation leads you to think before you speak, to formulate and organize your thoughts. Here you will also find new ways to cultivate the lost art of conversation, allowing you to be at ease in social situations, at meetings, and while networking.

Making the Journey—Entering into Public Speaking

In Part Two you will gain the tools and skills you need to enter into more public speaking situations. There is value in asking yourself, "What knowledge do I have that is important to share? How do I want my listeners to feel during and after my talk?" A step-by-step road map helps you organize, build confidence, and maximize effectiveness. Do you need practice managing "on-your-feet" situations, such as facilitating discussions, panels, and interviews? Do you wish you were better at fielding questions and coping with the media? You will learn to extend your skills to handle the unexpected, including difficult audiences. Here, too, are advanced techniques for events that call for persuasion, inspiration, or motivation, along with ideas that will help you to adapt your approach and style to the particular group you are planning to address.

Finishing Touches and Accessories

Now it's time to go forth and do it! In Part Three you will learn to inspire others by developing your delivery skills and your voice in order to project a vocal image of power and poise. Effective speaking relies on developing a relationship with the listener, and you will discover ways to move your body in order to capture the audience and command the situation. Understanding the uses of space, notes, and visual-media aids is an increasingly important part of speaking. You will acquire a toolbox filled with strategies for managing the environment in which you speak, for determining how and when to incorporate visual aids, microphones, and cameras, and for arranging your events to get the results you want.

BUILD ON YOUR OWN CHARISMA

Relax. You don't need to change who you are. Indeed, the key to successful communication is to be your best self, to let your self shine through. This book has many ideas and strategies, but the prime message is: You already possess people-skills and have important things to say. Just build on that. Trust yourself. The more you speak—every day—the better you will get at it, so prepare to shine. By the end of the book you will know how to Get **Ready** by managing your nervousness, then to **Aim** by forecasting and formulating. You'll be sure to **Inspire** with a delivery style that sizzles by speaking from your heart to your listener's eyes.

The invitation to speak can become a joyful opportunity to express yourself and improve yourself. Let every woman lift up her voice and be heard!

MANAGING NERVOUSNESS

Transform jitters into dynamic energy with these basic strategies to relax you and heighten your confidence

Nothing is a greater impediment to being
on good terms with others than being ill
at ease with yourself.
—HONORÉ DE BALZAC

Imagine picking up your phone messages one morning and finding that you have been invited to make a presentation about your pet project to an influential group of decision makers. Are you thrilled and raring to go, or terrified and praying you can find someone to take your place? Most likely you are experiencing both of these emotions. You are not alone. Remember *The Book of Lists*, which was based on surveys of thousands of Americans? It revealed that the number-one fear shared by most respondents was the fear of public speaking—above snakes, above high-rise fires, and above broken elevators. Yet we often feel alone in our discomfort and distress because everyone else we see speaking in groups appears calm, competent, and confident.

In the workshops that I offer, 99 percent of the participants say they feel nervous about coming to the front of the group to introduce themselves for a brief videotaped exercise. Yet once we finish the exercise and review the tape, they observe how calm, competent, and confident everyone appears, including them! They are surprised and relieved to find that butterflies are invisible. The audience does not sense the sweating palms, shaking knees and hands, quivering voice, thick tongue, or dry mouth. The exercise demonstrates that our bodily sensations are exaggerated and distracting only to us. They are ultimately irrelevant. We must learn to accept that these physical reactions are normal and move beyond them.

WELCOME THE BUTTERFLIES

The goal is to learn to manage nervousness, not to avert it. It is both natural and normal—and actually *useful*—to feel the jitters. Why is it useful? If you feel blasé about a presentation, how motivated will you be to prepare and push yourself to find creative ways to put forth your project? If you are nonchalant, you might be content just to show up and wing it. If you are completely calm, you might not be able to muster enough energy to make your presentation exciting and dynamic. Without nervousness you can become dull and uninspired. I have experienced this myself in my workshops. Sometimes my schedule demands that I present similar topics to similar audiences within a short period of time, which eventually leads me to go on autopilot. I do less preparation, just throwing the materials I need into my briefcase. Inevitably I start to feel bored and apathetic. Then I know it's time to introduce a new exercise that will challenge me and make me just nervous enough to inspire creativity.

Even in social situations, the nervousness you feel can be transformed into dynamic energy that puts a sparkle in your eye. Think of how you feel at the top of a challenging ski run. You've put a lot of effort and expense into getting there. You want to do it. Yet your heart is pounding. Your palms are clammy. You call it "a rush," "a thrill," "positive excitement." You can think of your speaking jitters the same way. Welcome, butterflies!

Nervous energy spurs us to greater creativity and a more animated delivery. The key is to prevent being *overcome* by nervousness, which can lead to a sense of panic and cause our thinking to become muddled. Stimulation increases effectiveness. Tension pushes us up out of the dull zone to a peak level of performance. But when we feel overwhelmed by nervousness, we begin to lose our fluency and train of thought, and our effectiveness decreases. We begin to fall into the panic zone.

How do we manage our nervousness to maximize its effectiveness and keep us at our peak performance level? There are two main avenues:

- The Body
- The Mind

CONTROL THE BODY

We need to cultivate the skill of sustaining a *calm body* with an *alert mind*. Many of us have forgotten, or have never known, how to achieve this balance. We are either awake, alert, and wired for action, or we are relaxed, lethargic, and possibly sleepy. Many of us take time to relax only when we are prepared to sleep.

With practice we can learn to maintain mental alertness while relaxing physically. The path to this state is through the breath. Breathing is the bridge between mind and body.

> **Exercise:** Let's try an experiment. Notice what happens to your breathing as you do the following: Look up to the left, then down to the right; repeat. Now look up to the right and down to the left; repeat. What happened to your breathing? Most likely you found that it almost stopped and became quite shallow.

We don't realize how we modify our breathing throughout the day (usually to the detriment of a full, life-sustaining breath). And when we do restrict our breathing in this way, we set off a cascade of physiological changes because the body is hardwired to respond to cues from the rate of respiration. Let's explore this concept through another experiment.

> **Exercise:** For the next 30 to 60 seconds, breathe rapidly and shallowly—the way you might start breathing when you hear that phone message inviting you to speak before the group of influential decision makers. Notice how you feel. What happens to the muscles in your body, your awareness of the room, peripheral vision, and hearing? What about your emotions? Try it now. Well? Did your muscles become tense and tight? Did your awareness narrow to the point where you felt conscious of your heart pounding and your mouth going dry? Did you feel as though you were in a tunnel with blinders on? And how did you feel emotionally? Most people report a feeling of anxiety, with a sense of doom or rising panic.

Amazing as it may seem, just by altering your breathing you have generated the *fight-or-flight reflex*. This reflex, also known as the stress response, is an integral part of the nervous system. It's like a red alert on a battleship; the lights flash, the buzzers sound, the loudspeakers announce "ATTENTION! THIS IS A RED ALERT; ALL SYSTEMS, ATTENTION; THIS IS AN EMERGENCY." The body cooperates with this warning by preparing for an emergency that requires a physical response: Either face the threat and deal with it, or get away from it as quickly as possible.

Such a physical reaction requires a quick response from the body's large muscles and a quick recovery time to help sustain the physical challenge. These responses set the nerves quivering. Moreover, a red alert calls for the shutting down of all nonessential functions, such as digestion and fine motor control of fingers, tongue, and facial muscles. Reasoning and problem-solving also become secondary in an emergency. We revert to Neanderthal logic—don't think; react. We are tight, tense, in a tunnel, and ready to run. In addition we feel queasy. Is this any way to give a speech?

The last thing we need to do in a speaking situation is to flee, and fighting is certainly not an option. What we do need is to bypass our reflexes and transcend our primitive reflexive brain, calling on our higher-level cerebral cortex. Controlling the breath allows us to shift quickly into the high-level mode. But it takes practice.

Use Your Breath to Stop, Center, Breathe, and Relax

Try another experiment.

> **Exercise:** Sit comfortably. This time, slow and deepen your breath, not so much by increasing the volume of breath (please don't hyperventilate!) but by increasing the depth. Breathe all the way to your belly button. Lengthen the exhalation. Imagine counting slowly to 4 for the inhalation; pause for a count of 3; exhale on a count of 4; pause for a count of 3; repeat. Do this for the next 30 to 60 seconds, or for about 6 breath cycles. Remember to place your attention on how you feel: muscles, awareness, emotions. Try it now. How do you feel? Most people report a sense of calm, with muscles much more loose and relaxed. Awareness of the room expands so that previously ignored sights and sounds enter the consciousness. This level of consciousness is the optimum state of being for a dynamic speaker.

With practice you can learn to use your breathing to help center and calm yourself before and during your presentations. To create these familiar and retrievable sensations in times of stress or nervousness, you need to practice and develop relaxation and breathing skills during noncritical times. Many techniques are available to help coax you into this state and to teach you the skills to achieve dynamic relaxation.

Yoga, meditation, T'ai chi, self-hypnosis, and other proven techniques help you learn to feel centered, grounded, and balanced. But specialized techniques are not really necessary. You can work on your own, just using the breathing exercises above, along with the relaxation exercises that follow.

Develop Relaxation Skills

Body tension is our reflexive response to stress, fear, or altered breathing. Healthy ways to release this tension do not come "naturally"; they take training and practice. Following are a few ways to induce a relaxed state. Tape-record the instructions so you can follow the exercises without reading. I like to close my eyes. Study the sensations these exercises generate and memorize them so you can call them up and replicate them at will:

• **Head rolls:** Sit comfortably with your spine straight, or stand with feet slightly apart, buttocks tucked in, and your spine relaxed, but straight. Drop your head to your chest. Feel the weight of it pulling down on your neck. Slowly roll your head in an arc until your left ear reaches your left shoulder; then bring it down to the center and roll it slowly over to the other side until your right ear reaches your right shoulder. Repeat several times, and feel the arc deepen as your head feels heavier and pulls the tension from your neck. (Avoid rolling your head back as this is injurious to the spine.)

• **Shoulder shrugs:** Lift both shoulders up as high as you can, until they practically touch your ears. Then let them drop. Notice how much lower they are. Repeat. Next, rotate each shoulder in turn in a clockwise circle about 10 times; then reverse and go counterclockwise.

• **Face:** Tighten all the tiny muscles of your face by grimacing and scrunching into funny faces. Curl your lips, sneer, frown, smile, move your mouth into a fish face and wiggle it from side to side, yawn, stretch, and then relax.

• **Rag doll, jaw wag:** While standing, bend forward from the waist. Keep your knees soft and everything relaxed with arms and head dangling and jaw relaxed. While hanging over, shake your head from side to side so that your loose jaw, lips, and face wag back and forth while you gently hum. (It sounds almost like gargling.) Then slowly begin to come back to standing by straightening one vertebra at a time so that your shoulders come up nearly last and then finally your head. Take a few deep breaths, and enjoy the luxurious feeling of relaxation. Repeat.

• **Progressive relaxation:** Work through each of the muscle groups in your body by tightening and then releasing the muscles, allowing each part of your body to fall back to a resting, supported position. Start by removing your shoes, and make sure you have enough room to extend your limbs and drop them comfortably. Sit restfully in a chair with eyes closed. Allow the chair to support you fully. Let your breath slow and deepen. First extend and tense your right leg—tight, tighter, as tight as you can. Flex the toes; feel the whole leg become stiff and so tight that it shakes. Then, let go completely. Feel your leg grow loose, limp, and relaxed. Now repeat with your left leg. Next, try your right arm. Make a fist; make the arm so tight that a weight could hang suspended from it. Then let it go. Feel your arm hanging, relaxed and loose. Now repeat with your left arm. Feel how your arms are as limp and relaxed as your legs. Next, contract your abdomen and buttocks by pulling in and squeezing. Release and feel the tension flow out. Now lift and tighten your shoulders (as for shrugs above). Then work on your neck, performing slow, easy head rolls (as described above). Finally, work on the face (see above). Scan your body with your mind and notice how loose and relaxed you feel. You may even feel heavy and warm. Spend a number of breath cycles enjoying the relaxed feelings. Memorize the sensations.

• **Autogenic relaxation:** Sit comfortably in a chair, with eyes closed. Allow the chair to support you. Let your breath slow and deepen. Now begin to work through each of the muscle groups in your body by imagining a golden light coming to each area. Imagine the warmth of the golden glow melting away all the tension. Begin with your toes. Imagine that golden light spreading slowly and deeply through your toes, the arch, and then the heel of your foot. The golden light moves up your ankles, to your calves, then your knees and thighs, melting away the tension. Next the light reaches your hips, abdomen, diaphragm, and chest. Your breath becomes deeper and slower, easier and more relaxed. The warm golden light now reaches your heart, hands, arms, and shoulders. Slowly, slowly, the golden light penetrates your neck, your face, your scalp. After the light has moved through your whole body, spend a number of breath cycles enjoying the relaxed feelings. Memorize the sensations.

The more you practice and deepen these skills on a daily basis the more likely you will be able to call them up while under the stress of a speaking situation. There are excellent tape recordings you can purchase to talk you through relaxation exercises. Some are listed in the Resources section at the end of the book. You can use these tools whenever you begin to sense the bodily sensations of the fight-or-flight response. Bypass this response by remembering to *Stop* (stop what you're doing), *Center* (check in with yourself), *Breathe* (slow and deepen your breathing), and *Relax* (remember the sensations you had in practice).

CONTROL THE MIND

The other route to getting out of the panic zone is the mind, as it is our *perception* of danger that triggers the fight-or-flight response. Speaking publicly and interacting socially pose no actual danger. You could search the records of local county courthouses for months and not find a single death certificate that shows "public speaking" as cause of death! Yet public speaking *seems* like a death-defying act. We must explore the underlying fears in order to contain them and render them manageable. When we shy away from fears and let them stay vague and general, they have great power over us. When we face them and identify them, they become challenges that we can meet with clear-cut solutions.

Identify Your Fears

What do we tell little children who are afraid of the bogeyman in the dark? "Turn on the lights, look under the bed, and open the closet door." When you open the door behind which your fear of public speaking is hiding, what exactly is in there?

> **Exercise:** Explore your fears of speaking by listing them. Get very specific by observing them from every angle. Are you afraid that you'll make a fool of yourself? How exactly would you do that? (Possible specifics: I'll leave out important information, mispronounce a name, be obviously nervous, not be able to answer a question, forget what I want to say.)

Once you list these specific fears, you can make specific plans to dispel them. For example:

• **I'll mispronounce a name:** Research and practice pronunciation of unfamiliar terms and names ahead of time. Keep your sense of humor; ask for the listeners' help.

• **I'll appear nervous:** Here are three ways to handle this fear.

1. Ignore physical symptoms of tension. Remember, the shakiness, clamminess, and dry mouth you feel do not show. Find an opportunity to videotape yourself so you can see for yourself how poised and calm you look in spite of your internal alarm.

2. Identify and eliminate any distracting habits you observe on that video, such as fidgeting, swaying, or pacing.

3. Understand and work with your particular physical responses. If you tend to blush or splotch dramatically, wear a high collar or scarf. If you perspire profusely, wear underarm protective pads. Work on slowing and deepening your breathing to minimize these symptoms.

• **I'll leave out important information:** Have an outline, handouts, and an overhead projector, or use a flip chart with the essentials to guide you and reinforce your content to the audience.

• **I'll be unable to answer all questions:** Do you know people who think they know it all? And how do you feel about them? Not very positively, right? So why do you want to be a know-it-all? Refer to Chapter 5 for ways to manage questions you can't answer. The best answer is the honest one: "I don't know."

• **I'll forget what I meant to say:** Similar to leaving out important information, so have an outline at hand. Give yourself permission to pause and review your notes, collect your thoughts, take a sip of water. The audience will be very forgiving and, indeed, appreciative of this evidence that you have a plan and are thoughtful.

Are you starting to get the idea? The more specific you can be about identifying your fears, the better prepared you can be to transform them into a specific plan of action. You will find that these concerns are actually valuable guideposts that stimulate thorough and creative planning, thereby preparing you to handle a range of contingencies. So whenever you feel a rush of adrenaline or fear, ask yourself: What is it that I am specifically worried about? How can I prepare for this?

Explore Your Fears

As you review your list of fears, you may find they fall into three general categories:

They: audience judgment
Mights: possible mistakes or problems
Shoulds: ego ideals and expectations

THEY WILL JUDGE ME

Is the audience a monster or a friend? We tend to anticipate our audience's disapproval and assume a negative response. But for the most part, audiences are empathetic and forgiving unless there is a particularly controversial issue involved. Why are they listening to you in the first place? Isn't it because they want to hear what you have to say? They want you to do well. Think back to a time when you heard a speaker who appeared nervous and unsure. How did you respond? You probably felt uncomfortable because you were empathetic: You began to feel what the speaker was feeling. For the sake of the audience, if not your own, *act as if* you feel comfortable. The person you will fool the most is yourself!

Audiences are also forgiving of mistakes if you make it easy for them and resist losing your composure. The key to poise is not perfection. You may make mistakes, and the important thing will be to recover gracefully. This you can do. Do you recall President Ford's stumble down the airplane stairs, or President Bush's stomach flu, or Senator Bob Dole's fall off the stage? Despite the exposure of international TV coverage, they recovered gracefully. So if you trip, or mispronounce a word, or spill a glass of water, you are in good company. Such mishaps are not important to the audience unless you make them so.

Resist drawing attention to your mistakes by apologizing, or by announcing them verbally or nonverbally (eye rolls, shoulder shrugs, tongue clucks, frowns). The listener may not even notice what you mispronounce or confuse. Develop the attitude, "I recover gracefully." Ignore what you can; use humor to minimize the rest. I have managed to keep talking with just a brief pause to retrieve a dropped note card. Or I've given a brief explanation while I tended to a logistical need: "Let me grab a fresh marker," or just, "Excuse me," while I turn aside to blow my nose.

SOMETHING *MIGHT* HAPPEN

The next group of fears centers on all the mishaps that *could* happen. The slide projector might not work; I might get a run in my hose; I might have spinach between my teeth; I might drop my notes and they might end up out of order. Guess what? You're right! These things might happen, so be smart and well prepared by anticipating common contingencies. Visit the site ahead of time to uncover potential problems. Familiarity will help prevent problems and boost your confidence. Have a spare projector bulb and a spare pair of pantyhose. Check your appearance. Number the pages of your notes and bind them. (Chapter 9 offers more suggestions for anticipating such contingencies.)

I *SHOULD* BE PERFECT

"I should be perfect," "I should be the best," "I should be scintillating." These are ego messages, and they are the most challenging mind tricks to tame. It is good to work toward excel-

lence—to be prepared, rehearsed, and polished. But doing well and achieving perfection are two very different things. We sabotage ourselves with high expectations. So an important part of the work of learning to speak in public is to train our minds to work *for* us, rather than *against* us.

Learn Mental Preparation Techniques

We have already learned the foundation—breathing! It is essential to establish the preconditions that foster mental training: *Stop, Center, Breathe,* and *Relax.* Alert mind, calm body. Once we use our breathing to center ourselves and achieve a receptive state, we can work on the mental training strategies.

TOOL #1: SELF-TALK

We tend to have a running conversation with ourselves, especially during stressful times. Become aware of your self-talk. Listen in and monitor it. What do you say to yourself about your ability to handle speaking situations? What are your predictions for success or failure? Sadly, most of us put ourselves down, drastically undermining our confidence in the process. Would you talk to a beloved friend the way you talk to yourself? You wouldn't? Then stop! Take control of your self-talk and make it work to support and prepare you.

Be a good coach to yourself. What does a good coach do? She encourages you. She believes in you. She gets you the training you need. She has high, yet attainable, expectations and offers constructive feedback. She names all your strengths, identifies strategies to overcome your weaknesses, and cheers you on. Do this for yourself.

Positive self-talk is a way to take charge of your nervous energy and channel it to positive uses. So when you find yourself saying to yourself: "Boy, what an idiot. Whatever made me think I could handle this challenge? I'll probably mess up and everyone will know. I'm too scared to do this. I'm not ready." — STOP this destructive chatter! Treat yourself as you would your dearest friend. Tell yourself: "I can do this. I'll just settle down and figure out what I need to do to get ready. I'll practice. I'll be patient. I can ask for help. And I'll learn from the experience."

TOOL #2: AFFIRMATIONS

We tend to fill our thoughts with self-fulfilling prophecies. How would you complete these sentences about yourself as a communicator and speaker?

> *I'm the kind of person who . . .*
> *I always . . .*
> *I never . . .*

These are affirmations, but are they affirming how you want to be or how you *don't* want to be? Remember Henry Ford's observation: "Whether you think you can or can't, you're right!" Affirmations can be a potent force to transform us— when we formulate them properly. The challenge is to compose them carefully so they help you become who you want to be. Here are a few basic principles to follow when creating affirmations:

• **Present tense:** "I *am* calm" instead of I will, could, or should, be calm.
• **Positive expression:** "I am *calm*," rather than "I'm not nervous."
• **Personal:** "*I* am calm," rather than "It is good to be calm."

Here are some of my favorite affirmations for public speaking: "*I am ready for this. People want to hear what I have to say. I have important and interesting things to say. I am calm and confident. I belong here."* Notice how different these positive affirmations feel, compared to "I'm not nervous," which contains a negative, or "I'll be ready," which is future tense, or "It's good to know your audience," which is impersonal. I repeat these affirmations like a mantra to manage my nervousness in the days before a presentation and on the day itself, while driving on my way to the presentation, while sitting and waiting to be introduced, and right up to the moment I begin to speak.

> **Exercise:** Review your list of fears and reframe each of them as strengths for yourself by formulating an affirmation. Examples:

fear:	reframed as affirmation:
I'm afraid I'll mispronounce someone's name.	I know how to pronounce peoples' names.
I'm afraid I'll forget what I want to say.	I remember what to say.
People will think I'm stupid if I can't answer all their questions.	I am comfortable saying "I don't know."

Check that each statement is positive, present tense, and personal. Keep each one short and direct.

TOOL #3: VISUALIZATION

Just as we carry on an inner conversation with ourselves, we run a continuous videotape in our minds. We picture how things will turn out. Research has shown that such visualization is effective in giving us experience, because the unconscious mind doesn't differentiate imagined from real practice.

Sports psychologists use this technique: If a player breaks her wrist and is unable to play for many weeks, she still goes out to practice—from the bench—in her imagination. When the cast is removed weeks later, the patterns and moves are still fresh in her mind. She has lost none of her knowledge and skills, although the muscles need to be strengthened and the tissue healed.

You can take advantage of this technique by imagining yourself giving your talk. The more you practice and the more vivid detail you bring, the more effective your visualization will be for improving your performance. What do you see? Is it a large room? What do you hear? Are the people silent, laughing, clapping? See and feel yourself moving around, gesturing, turning your head to scan the group. Include sensations of touch, smell, and taste, such as the cold glass of water in your hand and the coffee urn in the back of the room.

In the theater of your mind you can rehearse the most challenging moments you anticipate. It will help you build your skill and diminish your anxiety. For example, if you have a presentation on a controversial issue, imagine handling the audience's distress and objections with grace and finesse. (See Chapter 5 for further advice on handling difficult situations.) If you can't imagine accomplishing this, do some homework. Research, reflect, consult with others until you can imagine an effective way to handle the situation. Then mentally practice and polish your skill. Visualization provides a positive channel for the nervous energy that builds up in anticipation of a presentation, much as the mantra of affirmations does.

Do you experience intense blushing or red splotching on your face or neck? These symptoms may reflect your unconscious visualizations. You may be directing all the pent-up, excess energy generated by the beating wings of those butterflies up toward your face. So—pay attention to your feet! Visualize and say to yourself, "*I am firmly grounded. My energy moves down my body into the floor to root me and support me. My energy moves out into the audience to enliven them.*"

Visualization can also help with the aftermath of a presentation or conversation. If a situation does not go as well as you had hoped, what do you tend to do? Do you turn up the volume on all your "shoulds?" "I *should have been* perfect and scintillating." Do you continually replay the scene in your mind? This is, in fact, a mental rehearsal that reinforces doing it wrong! The "shoulds" keep you stuck in a past which you are helpless to alter. A better response to your post-presentation anxiety is to recreate the experience and transform it, rather than replay it. Imagine how you will do it differently *next* time: Rehearse every detail. Try this exercise:

Exercise: Think of a recent speaking situation that you would like to have handled better. Take time to get comfortable in your chair; breathe and relax. You may want to close your eyes. (*Note:* Record this paragraph in a calm and gentle voice, add in some of the details of your situation to coach you along, and then listen to it as a guide through the visualization.)

My breathing is even and slow as I begin to picture the scene . . . I can see the room and the people . . . I see myself speaking . . . As the situation unfolds, I see myself handling it very effectively . . . I feel calm and confident. My mind is clear and alert, my body is calm and relaxed as the scene continues . . . I hear my-self speaking clearly, strongly. It's going well. I feel good about how I am handling this. The others are responding positively. I remember to breathe. The scene continues . . . It's going well. I remember to breathe. I continue to follow the scene through . . . I know just what to say. I am managing this well . . . I take my time. I remain centered and confident. I am flexible and responsive. I competently handle all of the challenges . . . As I come to the end of the scene, I feel successful. My breathing is even and slow. I am ready to end the visualization. I wiggle my toes and wiggle my fingers, and when I am ready, I open my eyes.

How did it go? Were you able to envision success? You may have found that your scenario went well, up to a certain point. Perhaps you lost your concentration when someone interrupted you. Or you felt poised until you noticed your listener's frown. Were you able to visualize yourself recovering gracefully? If you were unable even to imagine it going well, it's time to do some homework again so that you can come up with an effective strategy. Talk to a friend, take a walk, and reflect on the situation. Reread some of the chapters in this book. As you develop a clear vision of how to be successful next time, you develop your poise and confidence.

These three mental training tools—positive self-talk, affirmations, and visualization—are powerful techniques to manage your nervousness. You can begin using them now, before any speaking opportunity arises. You can practice them as soon as you know you have a speaking situation coming up, in combination with preparation and practice.

TRANSFORM NERVOUS ENERGY

How much preparation and practice do you need? The answer depends on your own style and the particular level of demand or risk in each speaking situation. A friend of mine, who is somewhat introverted, refines, rehearses, and polishes even such informal speaking situations as opening small group discussions at our Sunday school's board/membership roundtable. This careful, thorough preparation helps her feel calm and articulate. I, on the other hand, am an extroverted, intuitive kind of person who feels most creative while in the midst of action. I like to talk, and I find that the act of talking helps me think. For me, preparation for low-keyed situations consists of thinking clearly about my goals, plus establishing a broad outline rather than fully scripting what I will say. Now that I have a lot of experience, I find I can limit preparation and practice to a minimum, even for more major talks, *if* I know the topic well. This bare-bones preparation always includes my opening and closing sentences, timelines, and transition based on clear objectives, with mental rehearsal focusing on audience response and the overall sense of my message.

Such a minimalist approach does not make sense when the topic is unfamiliar, for less experienced speakers, or for those more comfortable with a definite plan. The key is to find *your* way. When I face an unfamiliar topic or a more challenging audience, I increase the extent of preparation. For example, when I was invited to give a talk on "The Attorney's Voice" to senior members of the State Attorney General's Office at their annual convention, I found my butterflies multiplying to the extent that I chose to practice with an audience of invited friends before a video camera. Even though I had presented many similar workshops, I found that the high-level, unfamiliar audience made me uneasy. I even went out and bought an appropriate suit for the occasion. The extra preparation was well worth the effort as it gave me confidence and comfort. The talk went well, though I rarely wore that specially purchased red power suit again.

Can you begin to see how to vary your practice level? For those situations that are relatively positive, familiar, and comfortable you may choose to do your personal, minimum practice level. But whenever the occasion is higher on your "risk hierarchy," plan for more elaborate and thorough preparation.

Exercise: Map out your risk hierarchy for an upcoming speaking situation by ranking it according to the factors in Table 1:1 below. Then design your plan for preparation and practice accordingly, i.e., more extensive and elaborate planning for higher levels of risk.

| | **Level of risk:** | | | | |
| | easiest for me . . . . most difficult | | | | |
TABLE 1.1	1	2	3	4	5
relationship to listeners					
setting					
number of people present					
nature of topic					
receptivity to topic					
significance of event					
expectations					
other:					

Over the years, I have learned to "listen to my gut." Any time I begin to feel a surge of that queasy-with-butterflies sensation, I realize it's a gentle reminder that I need to *do* something to get ready. That's when I ask myself, "What is this nervousness attached to? What am I worried about? What exactly are my fears? What can I do to prepare for this possibility?" As soon as I come up with a plan of action, the butterflies begin to fly in formation, my nausea subsides, and a sense of upbeat anticipatory excitement takes over.

APPLY STRATEGIES TO MANAGE NERVES

Here are some additional strategies to help you on the actual day and at the very hour of the presentation. First and foremost, keep yourself in balance. Get the exercise your body needs. Take a brisk walk just before your presentation whenever possible. Make sure you are well rested. Eat wisely and lightly. Have water handy, but don't drink too much, and avoid carbonated drinks. Dress in something that boosts your confidence. Arrive early to insure everything is in order—seating arrangements, equipment, projector bulbs, lighting. (There are numerous suggestions in Chapter 9.) Give yourself plenty of time. Save time for going to the restroom. Use the mental training techniques vigorously: *Stop, Center, BREATHE, Relax.* Check in with your good "coach." Activate positive self-talk, affirm, visualize, BREATHE. Adapt my mantra to suit you: *"I am ready for this. People want to hear what I have to say. I have important and interesting things to say. I am calm and confident. I belong here."*

Just before you're introduced, while on the sidelines, continue to focus on the mental training strategies. Keep your body relaxed so that you don't contract into a tight ball. Uncross your legs and wiggle your toes to make sure your leg doesn't go to sleep. Let your arms dangle and shake your fingers loosely to relax and get the blood flowing. Imagine a loved one standing before you, gently pushing down on your shoulders and giving you a loving kiss on the forehead. Do a few subtle jaw wags to loosen your jaw. Smile and say *mm 'hmm* as you listen rapturously to the speaker before you in order to relax your face and warm up your voice. And—you guessed it—breathe, breathe, breathe! Take slow, deep, expansive, cleansing breaths. Fill your mind with your affirmations. *"I am ready for this."*

As your moment approaches, BREATHE! Take your time.

Use your breath to slow yourself down. As you reach the front of the room and face the audience, take time to get yourself grounded and calm. Smile as you look around. BREATHE. Do not feel compelled to start talking. Wait to begin until you can notice your surroundings. Focus on the tangible environment for a moment until you can see the texture in the carpet, the wood grain of the table, the smile of that friendly person in the third row, the beautiful pattern of her blouse. Use this time to look around and begin connecting with your audience through eye contact and smiling. Mentally repeat your mantra. Imagine yourself speaking with power, poise, and presence. Take another moment to breathe. Center and calm. All this will help you begin from a place of balance and grounded power. When you sense this grounded feeling you are ready to commence. Fill your mind with the mental training tools. Allow no room for undermining doubts and fears. Tell yourself, "*I belong here. I am ready for this. I am excited and in control.*" Breathe.

Now you may begin dynamically, totally confident, totally in control. Even if you are bluffing, the person you will persuade most convincingly is yourself! You can do it! Ignore any sensations of jitters. Your polished and practiced opening will help launch you. Once you are off to this strong start and coach yourself through the first critical moments, you will find that the momentum carries you through.

If, after a few minutes, you begin to lose that grounded feeling, take a moment to pause and reground yourself. You have probably restricted your breathing unwittingly. BREATHE. Keep managing your internal dialogue and recall your affirmations. Speak only when you are in touch with your higher-level cerebral cortex. Pause if you begin to sense you are entering the tunnel of reactive fight-or-flight. Light-headedness or tightening of the throat are symptoms of poor breathing. *Stop*, *Center*, *Breathe*, and *Relax*. Take a sip of water. Review your notes. The audience is tolerant of such pauses. Indeed, later chapters show that there are benefits to pauses.

You know how to manage your nervousness. You are poised and powerful. You use the butterflies to energize your delivery. You remember to breathe. Accept that invitation to speak!

EVERYDAY IMPROMPTU SPEAKING

How can you prepare for the unexpected?

You've learned ways to manage nervousness for the anticipated speaking situations. How can you prepare for the unexpected? Spontaneous does not need to mean unprepared or uninformed. You can begin to approach all situations as opportunities to speak and thus learn to forecast and formulate where you want to go and how you want to get there. As the actress Ruth Gordon once said, "The best impromptu speeches are the ones written well in advance." Preparing ahead allows you to take advantage of, and enjoy, unexpected opportunities.

FORECAST THE SITUATION

Consider the next gathering you will attend. What opportunities might it present for speaking? Will people be present who can further your favorite cause or project? What issues or topics might be discussed? Here's an example:

Imagine you have been a volunteer for the past three years at the Help Hotline Center. This morning you are on your way to a training session for the new crop of volunteers. True, your role today will be limited, as you have agreed only to help serve coffee and bagels at the break, but surely there will be informal questions and discussions at the snack table. You might even be asked to make a comment before the group. Begin to forecast and formulate so you will feel fortified. Spend your travel time to this session mentally preparing. Focus your brainstorming on these key strategies:

Anticipate: What questions, requests, or issues may come up?
Clarify: What are your goals and objectives? Why would you speak? What would you like to have happen in terms of outcomes, results, or actions?
Customize: Who will your listeners be? Why would they want to listen?
Consider the Context: What is the setting?

At this hotline training session, you anticipate that the new volunteers will probably want to know about your experiences—the best ones and the worst ones. They'll want to know how much of a time commitment volunteering requires, and what the rewards and problems have been for you. As you answer their questions, what are your goals? You want to encourage the new volunteers and help them prepare for the challenges. What are their needs? They need to feel reassured that this program is worthy of their efforts and that they are capable of carrying out the responsibilities. The context is a task-oriented training session, with emphasis on community service and leavened with a light socializing touch since this is strictly a voluntary endeavor.

As you think about these possibilities on your way to the training session, you will want to recall interactions that illustrate the value you place on the hotline and how much you have appreciated the experience. Think back to your early days, and you will remember your initial concerns and some of the lessons you learned. These memories will help you imagine how you will answer some of the questions that may come up.

TAKE TIME TO THINK ON YOUR FEET

When you are put on the spot and asked to respond quickly, take a moment or two to organize your thoughts. Where do you want to go with this? What's the best way to get there? The request put before you is not like the starting gun at a race-track. You can pause and take time to think. Don't worry about keeping your listener waiting. She will be positively impressed with the thoughtfulness you are giving to her request. Avoid letting your mouth work faster than your brain. You don't want to say anything you haven't thought out!

There are ways to "buy" time for formulating an answer. You can, for example, repeat or rephrase the question or request: *"You would like me to talk about how I felt in the first weeks covering the hotline and how I managed calls when feeling less experienced?"* You can comment on the request. *"I'm so glad you asked." . . . "This is a very important issue for us to consider." . . . "Yes, I would very much like to speak about this, as I think it is critical for the new volunteers."* You can state the need to reflect. *"That's a key question. Let me think about it for a moment."* Or you can indicate in nonverbal ways that you are preparing your thoughts: look up with raised eyebrows, tap your chin, straighten your notes, or sip some water. In the meantime, your brain is working away at thinking through your response. It takes only 15 percent of your brain to attend to what is said to you and to make semiautomatic responses. That leaves 85 percent of your thinking capacity for formulating answers. The key is to use this brainpower to plan and ponder, not to panic.

Are you an extrovert or an introvert? If you are an extrovert like me, you do your best thinking by talking. Sometimes the only way you know what you think is by talking it out. Your energy and creativity are stimulated and renewed through interacting with the external world. The challenge extroverts face is to avoid talking before—even without—thinking. If you leap into the conversation without thinking, you might end up somewhere you never intended, lost without a map. Remember to pause and take just a few moments to think, so that you can express yourself more effectively.

Introverts, on the other hand, get their energy and creativity from a private inner source. They do their best thinking while alone and are reticent to express their thoughts. They want to have every detail worked out perfectly before responding, and by then either someone else has expressed the thought, or the moment has passed. The challenge for introverts is to learn to respond more quickly, with an approximate rather than a precise road map.

Both extroverts and introverts benefit by remembering to use the mental training tools described in Chapter 2. *Stop, Center, Breathe, Relax.* Use positive self-talk, affirmations, and visualizations, and you'll be able to think clearly and respond quickly.

Formulate Your Responses

Use a simple organizing pattern for formulating extemporaneous remarks. The acronym MRS. P. can serve as a guide. Mrs. P. will help bring you power, poise, and presence.

M   Message
R   Reason
S   Support
P   Propel

MESSAGE

Where do you want to go with your comments? What is your main point? The key is to begin with a plan. Wait to begin speaking until you know what you want your ultimate message to convey. Choose this focus according to your listener's needs: remember to *clarify* and *customize*. Avoid hedging or overqualifying what you say. Choose your point and go for it, so that you can be focused, definite, and succinct.

REASON

Why have you chosen this point of view? Give reasons to support your opinion. Structure your key points in some way, for example by enumerating them: *"I see three issues here."* Another way to structure is to state the problem as you see it and offer your solution: *"It seems to me the real problem is a financial one. Here's what I think we can do to make more money."* Or you can outline the issue according to chronology: *"Let me explain the history of the organization and where I think we are going."*

SUPPORT

What evidence and examples amplify your position? Provide anecdotes, case histories, or personal experience, as well as facts or statistics to back up your opinion. Make your stories inspiring. Be brief!

PROPEL

What do you want the listener to do as a result of your position? What action can people take? Engage your listener with a clear call to action. Then end firmly with a restatement of your message. Resist the impulse to ramble. The greatest challenge in impromptu situations is to stay focused and succinct.

If you remember these steps, MRS. P. will help you focus, organize, and deliver a strong succinct message. Extroverts— Don't begin speaking before you have a clear road map that leads to the conclusion. Target the essential message and keep in mind why you are speaking and how you will attain the desired results. Introverts—You are ready to begin once you have chosen the message, determined your goal in speaking, and identified supportive evidence. Trust yourself to flesh out the wording and transitions.

Find a way to open strongly so that you will "hook" the listener and make her receptive to your discussion. Do this by framing your message from the *listener's* point of view according to her needs and interests. There is a saying that the first things said are more important than the next ten thousand.

How would this formula fit with our example of the training session at the hotline? Imagine yourself saying something like this, using the problem-solution approach: "Like many of you, I wondered how I could possibly take a shift on the hotline without having a great deal of experience." (**Message**) "Yet how could I get experience without diving in? It was like the proverbial chicken/egg question. So I decided to dive in and give it a try." (**Reason**) "I was terrified. But with each call I found my confidence growing, and I came to realize that most calls are quite routine, with people asking for referrals and resources. When more challenging calls came through, I struggled as best I could, remembering the training and trusting my intuition. I went over these calls with senior staff before I left for the day. Their feedback reassured me that I had handled the situations satisfactorily. I reminded myself that there never is a perfect way to do it, nor is there a formula to follow." (**Support**) "I think you can do it. Trust yourself and you will see yourself grow in skill and confidence." (**Propel**)

As with any skill, the more you practice, the better you will get. Try this exercise alone or, for fun, take turns with a few friends.

Exercise: Write a list of topics, words, and/or quotes, each on a separate strip of paper. Place the strips in a box or bowl and draw one out. Give yourself 10 to 20 seconds to prepare. (With practice, you can get this down to 5 seconds.) Once your thoughts are organized, particularly in terms of your primary message, begin to speak out loud. (Tape yourself whenever possible.) Speak for 30 to 60 seconds or so.

How did you do? Evaluate your response as you ask yourself the following: Did I stay focused? Find a strong opening and closing? Offer inspiring reasons and examples to support my thoughts? Use vivid language? Organize in some fashion? Find a way to propel the listener to action? End firmly? Breathe, center, calm?

Now try the same topic again, with greater focus.

Practice the Unexpected!

Opportunities for practice arise every day. First, you can mentally rehearse. When? Agatha Christie once said, "The best time for planning a book is while you're doing the dishes." The same holds true when preparing for impromptu situations. Next, you can try structuring and polishing your remarks in your next conversation, even when the topic is as common and everyday as a favorite TV show or book, or when you are discussing current events at the dinner table. Take 10 seconds to come up with your hook-opening and propel-closing, and allow yourself 20 seconds to come up with your main reasons and evidence. For example:

"I have a favorite book that showed me how to transform my frustrations and anger into usable energy. The book is *Warriors of the Heart* and it is by my greatest mentor, Danaan Parry. I gain new insights and resolve each time I leaf through it. Danaan filled this book with personal awareness exercises, illuminating anecdotes, and practical instruction in the art of conflict resolution drawn from his work among such combatants as the Catholics and Protestants in Ireland. Read it. I know that you'll be inspired."

Or, for another example, a woman might say to her husband, "We sound tired and disgruntled with this universe. I need to explore other galaxies tonight, how about you? Let's get some otherworldly inspiration and watch "Voyager" together. It's a new episode that's supposed to be amusing with an upbeat message. We'll relax and keep each other company. It will do us both a world of good, don't you think? And I'll make the popcorn!"

Now you can try out this approach in real-life situations. Let's imagine you are at a PTA meeting, and you want to contribute to the discussion on the use of videos and TV in the classroom. **Forecast** (Anticipate, clarify, and customize): Your audience will be made up of parents and teachers who share your commitment to maximizing their children's learning and growth. **Formulate** (Gather the elements of MRS. P. You may want to vary the order by beginning with the conclusion-propel and then backing it up): "Teachers should restrict their use of videos. Out of school, most of our children spend far too many hours glued to the TV. The classroom is an opportunity for them to interact with each other under the guidance of the teacher." Or you can begin with your reasons and support, and offer the conclusion-propel last: "Studies show that our children spend an extraordinary number of hours passively glued to the TV. Since the classroom offers an opportunity for interaction and guidance, I believe teachers should restrict their use of videos in the classroom."

As you practice crafting your remarks, your confidence and pleasure will soar. Rehearsal and repetition will help you develop mental habits of forecasting and formulating. Your heart will still beat faster, but you will welcome this rush of adrenaline as a positive stimulant. So take the initiative whenever you can!

CULTIVATE THE ART OF CONVERSATION

Our lives are filled with occasions where we need to engage in conversational give-and-take with individuals outside our circle of family, friends, and colleagues. We travel aboard trains, planes, and buses. We sit next to strangers at banquets and weddings. We go to meetings, open houses, auctions, church socials, conferences, and receptions. We walk into a room where people are clustered in small groups, chatting away. It can take an act of courage to approach such a gathering with confidence and poise. But if you find people at all interesting, and enjoy listening, you already have what it takes to become an excellent conversationalist.

Some say conversation is a lost art. It needn't be lost on you. The same strategies I have suggested for impromptu speaking will help you revive your own conversational skills and inspire others to speak in depth about subjects that interest you and them. By approaching each interaction with forethought and attention, you can reduce anxiety, present your best self, and learn what others have to offer.

Recall the tools you learned to manage nervousness. **Stop** (You are safe and can handle this). **Center** (Eliminate your negative self-talk). **Breathe** (Slow and deepen your breath). **Relax** (Call up those rehearsed feelings of inner tranquillity). Negative self-talk is the cause of much nervousness in a social situation. Here is what you need to do if you find it a problem:

Fire the Judge:	Hire the Coach:
I never know what to say.	I show my enjoyment in others.
I'll be boring.	I have many interests.
No one will want to talk to me.	I can make the first move.
I always say dumb things.	I ask stimulating questions.

Dress Up Your Mind

Next, convert the strategies of forecasting and formulating we used for impromptu speaking to fit social events:

- **Anticipate:** What is the occasion? What kinds of opportunities and expectations will there be for interacting? Is the situation structured so that interactions might be limited to the people seated near you, or will there be opportunities to mingle? Who will be there? Is there anyone in particular you want to meet? Will the host be likely to make formal introductions, or will you be on your own?
- **Clarify:** What goals and objectives do you have? Do you want to make new friends, establish a reputation, make business contacts, or just have fun?
- **Customize:** What are the others like? What are their backgrounds? Their expectations and motivation for attending? What potential for common ground is there?
- **Consider the Context:** What is the setting and overall ambience?

Let's apply this plan to a typical scenario. You have been invited to the annual open house of your significant other's company. There will be more than fifty people at the no-host reception. The setting will be elegant, since the company has reserved the penthouse of the newest hotel in town. You wisely decide to wear something that makes you feel gorgeous.

While you are getting ready for the gathering, you take the time to prepare mentally, dressing up your mind while you put on your makeup. You anticipate milling crowds with lines at the bar and the buffet table. Your significant other loves to network and is likely to disappear within the first five minutes. Your primary goal is to enjoy the evening, perhaps put in a good word for your partner and meet several of the people you have heard about. You decide to ask your partner to introduce you to those special few, and you go over their names until they are firmly in your mind.

You consider that the other guests will also be ready for a good time mixed with a healthy dose of networking. They are a young, well-educated, and ambitious group, so you decide to take a few minutes before you leave to scan the newspaper and think about current topics of interest. By now you are likely feeling more at ease and actually looking forward to the evening. You have everything you need to sustain several conversations.

The Dance of Conversation

The give-and-take movement of conversation is a lot like dancing. First you need to find a partner. How do you break in? In the old days, there were dance cards to structure the shuffle of partners. Nowadays you have to devise your own ways. On a dance floor, you would probably be drawn to join groups engaged in free form or line dancing, but would avoid couples enjoying sultry slow dancing or four couples preparing for a square dance.

You can make similarly appropriate selections in a room filled with people talking and interacting. Observe the groups. Pay attention to body language—do they look open and receptive? Seek those who are having fun and laughing. Approach them, and stand in proximity. You can ask directly, "Excuse me, mind if I jump in?" Or make a comment, "Whoa, that must have been a great story, from the grins on all your faces. You look like a friendly group, may I join you?" Or just stand at the edge of the circle, become an active listener, and eventually make a remark.

Resist staying with only one person or one group in one area the whole time you are at an event. Circulate. Seek other people who are looking around the room, ready for a change in partners. Catch their gaze. Smile. Approach. You are ready to dance to a new beat.

KEEP THE BANTER UPBEAT AND LIGHT

When you enter the room, visualize yourself broadcasting a clear signal: "I am approachable and friendly. I put others at ease." Not only will others be attracted and pleased, but you too will feel at ease and enjoy the interactions. Some people say being a good conversationalist is like being a good lover. Be responsive and considerate, and make your partner feel irresistible and charming. Try openers such as, "I hear you're a whiz at . . ." or, "Could you show me how to . . ." or, "I'd love to know more about your interest in . . ."

These initial encounters thrive on easy, upbeat topics and flounder in gloom-and-doom or controversy. Before you know a person well, it's best to avoid mentioning the failing economy, the decay of civilization, and health or money problems; and keep clear of the land mines of religion and politics. Above all, don't be judgmental, negative, or a know-it-all. When in doubt, remain in the pleasurable realms of leisure and entertainment—movies, books, food, hobbies, travel, sports, music, and the arts.

Small talk has a bad reputation. Many sneer that it is petty, a waste of time, dull. Yet let's consider the valuable outcomes of effective small talk. Through it the participants build rapport, develop confidence, and establish building blocks essential for developing a relationship. As in romance, small talk prepares the way for more involved interaction. Both parties can move beyond first impressions by identifying common interests and language. In this regard, the feminine style of communication reigns supreme. While many men are prone to use language to establish their worth in a hierarchical sense, women are more likely to use language to gain consensus and collaboration. At ease with their intuition, many women develop a proclivity for constant communication in order to gain consensus and preserve trust. This creates a "communicative community," which many men perceive as "chatter" and pejoratively label as gossip. Women, too, are susceptible to putting down these interactions, calling them "just girl talk."

It's important for women to resist succumbing to the notion that intimate talk is frivolous, and to continue to offer support, respect, and attention to each other in mixed groups. Times are changing. Hierarchies are tumbling down; authority is in retreat. It has become clear that linear problem solving doesn't work as well as it once did. In the face of these challenges, ongoing communication is just what is needed. The feminine style of communication creates bonds that empower people in new ways.

So, even at the company open house, you can be the catalyst for a successful interaction by making the first move and creating a safe and comfortable climate that invites mutual interest. As you begin a conversation, play off cues you find in your surroundings. Here are some possible openers:

• (You find yourself next to someone in the buffet line) "This food looks great. I wish I could find a cozy neighborhood restaurant that serves pasta that looks this good. Do you have any recommendations? (After a reply) I do know of a great little Greek place. . . ."

• (You're near a window) "The sky is so gorgeous this evening. It makes me think of some of the wonderful sunsets I've seen on my travels. Where have your favorites been? (After a reply) I remember one down in the Keys. . . ."

• "I love the colors in this room. They would make a magnificent quilt. Have you ever made a quilt? (After a reply) I am just in the designing stage for something called a watercolor quilt. What kind of crafts do you like to do?"

• (You notice a trophy) "Have you ever played golf? I haven't, but I am feeling so inspired by the stories about Tiger Woods that I just may give it a try. Have you been following his career?"

• (There's music in the background) "I keep hearing about the Celtic music and dance craze. Have you seen *RiverDance*? (After a reply) Can you recommend any CDs? What kind of music do you like?"

• "Have you had a chance to read the autobiography of Katherine Graham? (After a reply) What an amazing story for a woman in this decade. I used to fantasize about working in journalism. Do you like to read? What kind of books? (After a reply) I'd love some recommendations."

Develop a repertoire of your own favorite personal stories, which you can craft and fine-tune over time. Just be sure not to tell them too often to the same listener! Think of such unusual, funny, fascinating moments as:

• a mix-up in date or time
• a blind date
• embarrassing moments
• an unusual party
• an amazing coincidence
• the weirdest gift
• an extraordinary mentor

FOCUS ON YOUR CONVERSATION PARTNER

Most people thrive on attention and enjoy talking when they have the luxury of a good listener. So offer your ears! Develop the art of asking open-ended questions and you will be rewarded with willing conversation partners. The value of an open-ended question is that it elicits a complex response, as opposed to a closed question, which will elicit just a single word or two. For example, "What's it like living here?" is open-ended. "Do you live here?" is closed. Consider, "Tell me about your work" versus "What do you do?" or "How did you get to know our host?" versus "Have you known our host long?"

In the mixer situation, pose open-ended questions that ask about your partner's interests, concerns, feelings, background, and experiences.

• "Tomorrow is supposed to be a gorgeous, sunny day. How do you like to spend the day when the weather is good?"
• "What are your thoughts on how this new civic center can benefit our community?"
• "What kinds of experiences have you had with other organizations that you've volunteered for?"

Once you pose a question, you need to listen closely to the answer so that you can ask follow-up questions in order to continue the conversation. Listen for content and feelings that may be expressed through nonverbal signals. Be interested, receptive, positive, and nonjudgmental, and you will gain a reputation as a superb conversationalist.

Here again, the challenge and opportunities are different for extroverts and introverts. The extrovert needs to remember to LISTEN as well as to tell her own fascinating stories. She is comfortable taking the initiative, so her challenge as a conversationalist is to draw others out and make *them* feel comfortable, too.

The introvert is already a good listener, but she must compel herself to approach and engage people with questions that keep a conversation going. Being a good listener goes beyond keeping silent while someone else speaks. The introverted person's challenge is to surrender self-consciousness by focusing on her partner and then actively contributing so that the conversation does not reach a dead end too soon.

The dance of conversation can come to a complete halt when partners' listening styles reflect gender differences. When your listener looks attentive, nods her head, and murmurs *mm 'hmm*, most women translate it as meaning "I am listening, I am interested, please continue." But men translate the nods and murmurs as meaning "Yes, you are right, I agree." Witness the birth of many misunderstandings! If the listener continues this responsive murmuring, male speakers might begin to interpret it as a condescending "Yeah, yeah, get on with it," and will either shut down or get defensive, whereas a woman listener may feel encouraged to continue and elaborate.

What does it mean when a listener looks you in the eye and is absolutely silent and still? Women often interpret this response as "Hurry up. I'm not really interested. You are boring me," and so they tend to shut down or change the topic. Yet male listeners offer this stillness—and interpret it—as active attention and listening. The lesson to us as conversationalists is: assume nothing! Check it out. I am learning to ask, when my stomach churns in response to my male listeners' apparent nonresponsiveness, "Are you interested? Shall I continue?"

MAKE IT EASY FOR YOUR PARTNER

Make it easy for your partner to engage in conversation by responding and volunteering information once things get started. Highlight and build on any commonalities you discover by making remarks and asking follow-up questions. It is unfair to expect the other person to carry the conversation. Help her out. Share experience; take turns. Offer stories and anecdotes. Express your point of view and show your interest and enthusiasm for the exchange. When you answer, offer more than a single word or, worse, a nonverbal nod or grunt. The more you reveal yourself—your thoughts, feelings, and experiences—the more the relationship can develop.

Generate energy by asking questions and initiating topics. But also relax; allow some silence. Often a period of silence means that your partner is formulating a thoughtful question for you or preparing to answer your questions in more depth. As the conversation progresses, more topics can be explored. Make it a policy to read the newspaper and current magazines, watch TV specials, and check the Web to keep yourself informed. Then you can express an educated opinion while remaining open and receptive to other perspectives.

Here are some possible next steps to the three conversation starters above:

• (Sunny day) I love to go hiking, too. Where are your favorite places? (After a reply) I just went on an Audubon Society outing and began learning about bird watching. Have you ever? Would you like to find out about their trips?

• (New civic center) "I agree, teens really need safe and positive environments. I hear they're planning to set up a sound system so they can have dances. They're looking for some equipment. What do you think of hooking up the teens with the senior center?"

• (Other volunteer experiences) "What does that organization do? I bet you have some great stories. I once hosted a foreign student, too."

Keep in mind that people like to talk about their families, their pets, their skills, and their occupations or avocations. Ask questions about your partner's strengths; pay a compliment; find common ground. Ask bicyclists their counsel on equipment. Encourage runners to tell their marathon stories. If you are still uneasy, bring something along to share. How about a Dilbert cartoon? A quote by Bill Gates? A photo or a special piece of jewelry can serve as a conversation piece.

During this dance of conversation, remember to make it

easy for your partner. Find common interests so you can swing to the same music. Follow a rhythm of listening and telling, asking and disclosing. Don't abandon your partner in the middle of a song. Lead into the next step and add some new moves. Avoid one-word responses—they are as irksome and deadly as coming to a standstill in the middle of dipping your partner. Instead, respond and react, add and reflect, volunteer information with grace and energy. As with all activities and exercise, the more you do it, the easier it gets and the more fit and skilled you get. You will find it is a lot more fun to dance than to hang on the sidelines like a wilting wallflower.

Negotiate the Sticky Situations

Sometimes the problem isn't getting yourself to join in the dancing, but getting *away* from a difficult or tiresome partner. How do you disengage?

- Begin to speak in the past tense: "It's been nice talking to you."
- Tell your partner graciously but directly that you are moving on: "I see someone I have wanted to check in with. Have a good evening." If she persists, patiently say again, "Thanks again, but I really need to go."
- Use nonverbal cues. Stop offering eye contact, begin moving away, and raise your hand slightly with the palm toward the person you want to leave.
- For the really tough cases, there is always the little white lie: "Excuse me, I have to go to the bathroom."

Unwanted personal questions present another challenge. These can often be gracefully sidestepped. When your father asks, with a wincing look, "How much did you pay for that?" you can state expansively, "I got a great deal; would you like the store's number?" If your neighbor probes, "How did you vote on that proposition?" you can reply, "It was a tough call. Your roses look magnificent, by the way. What fertilizer are you using?" A friend pries, "What was Janet so upset about?" You respond, "I'm not comfortable sharing her news, but I'd love to tell you mine." If your inquisitor persists, you can be direct but gracious by replying, "It feels really special that Janet places enough trust and value in me to confide. It's because I honor that trust that I have such special friends like you and Janet."

There are other times when you find yourself interacting with the latest incarnation of Don Imus or David Letterman. What do you do with sarcasm or with statements that might be interpreted as insulting? Above all, keep your sense of humor and don't get hooked. Breathe deeply. Imagine an invisible shield around you, keeping you safe. Picture the offending person at the wrong end of a telescope, looking small, pathetic, and rather silly while she is making her sarcastic remarks. The less you respond, the less you feed their disagreeable wisecracks. Think of yourself as a free fish that does not have to bite, no matter how provoking and enticing the bait. Remember, anglers change ponds when there's nothing biting.

Enhance the Quality of Everyday Conversation

Good conversation can develop beyond small talk into quality communication, given the right time and place, an attitude of openness, and freedom from judgment. Active and supportive listening, coupled with the generous use of self-disclosure, will help this development. Author Brenda Ueland wrote: "When we are listened to, it creates us, makes us unfold and expand. Ideas actually begin to grow within us and come to life." This kind of listening requires a flexible mind and an open heart. Yet often when we think we are listening, we are merely holding our tongue while gathering ammunition for our rebuttal. The quality of everyday speaking will improve as we learn to step into the role of listener to hear and understand from our partners' point of view, rather than to refute what they say or convert them to our own position. Once we understand their perspective, we can take our turn to offer our point of view.

When you get to the stage in a conversation where it is appropriate to express opinions or enter into a light debate, learn to frame your comments from your point of view as *I*-statements rather than *you*-statements. An *I*-message emanates from yourself and provides a direct statement about your observations or requests. It does not deal with assumptions, motives, or judgments. In contrast, a *you*-statement places blame and implies intention. Contrast the following: *"I don't understand"* versus *"You're confusing me." "I disagree"* versus *"You're wrong." "I'd rather not say"* versus *"You have no right to ask."* Can you see how the *I*-statements open a door for your message to be heard, whereas the *you*-statements slam it shut?

The trick in coping with someone who is trying to "hook" you is to avoid becoming defensive. The same tools you use for managing nervousness will serve you here. For example, when my teenage daughter starts to hook me with a negative comment, I try to remember to **Stop** (check my self-talk: *"She is not a 'rotten kid,' just an adolescent; I am not a basket case, just a hardworking mother"*). **Center** (chant my mantra of affirmations: *"I am a patient mother"*). **Breathe** (visualize a happy ending to the interchange: We finish with a hug). **Relax** (remember, next time can go even better).

NETWORK FOR SURVIVAL

Impromptu speaking is the most useful skill for networking. While you might think networking is just for ambitious career people, it is actually a vital tool for survival, given the way we live today. When your neighbors and family members go to far-flung schools, churches, and jobs, it is dangerously easy to become isolated in contemporary life. But you can *create* community by weaving a web of connections through communication. By learning to network effectively, you can gain the support and resources you need.

Last year I was at a luncheon with several hundred people. The guest speaker led us through an exercise to demonstrate how almost any resource is only four or five people away from us. We were invited to submit cards with any need we had, anywhere in the world. For example, I was looking for a housesitter for Thanksgiving, and a tablemate was trying to find a lost relative in a small town in Alabama.

As the leader read the submitted cards, we in the audience signaled whenever we thought we had a lead or a resource. I offered leads to three people. One was looking for a preschool for her children, one wanted a contact in Los Angeles for dance lessons, and one needed a tax accountant (work for my husband!). Locating the lost relative took a little digging, but we were able to find someone with a cousin who lived in that town. And I left with a juicy list of prospects for a housesitter. I was amazed at the power of networking for all our needs. Research has proven that we can connect with anyone on the planet when we activate our network and traverse those four to six "global stepping stones."

Networking involves a lot of give-and-take. Think of your own resources, skills, and experience; consider how you might serve others and offer your help. Are you creative, organized, sympathetic? Do you have a seven-passenger car? Are you a good editor or diplomat? Identify what it is you need: physical resources? social interaction? computer support? emotional objectivity or support? professional contacts or referrals? Next, think about who is in your network and how they can be a valuable resource for you. Ask for and use their support. You will be surprised to discover how vast your web of connections is, from the dentist to the corner grocer, book-club friends, former colleagues, past high school teachers.

Where do we begin when we don't have a banquet room full of people? The possibilities are vast. First there are the events practically designed for networking, such as church socials, company parties, conventions, conferences, and lunch meetings. But what about waiting in line at the supermarket or post office? Checking in with the receptionist at your dentist's office? Bumping into fellow shoppers at the garden store? The people in the next lane at the bowling alley? Your aerobics class? Be prepared for the opportunities that come up by *anticipating*. All of these situations become networking opportunities if you are willing to break the ice and engage in speaking.

Breaking the ice becomes enjoyable if you expect and plan for an approach. Build on the openers described for conversational situations. Think of extending a remark or a question as you would a warm, friendly handshake. Aim to put people at ease and reach out to them. Offer your name. If you met before, remind your partner of the circumstances and your name in case her memory falters.

Introduce Yourself with Pizzazz

Practice introducing yourself in a catchy way in less than 15 seconds. Offer enough information to show your uniqueness and intrigue the listener. Here's one option I've used: "I'm a coach for the workplace. I give workshops to help individuals handle time and stress better, and to improve their work relationships. I lead retreats to help groups become winning teams." This concise but complete answer tells more than a pedestrian "I'm a training and management consultant," and it gives your partner more to go on if she wants to continue the conversation. Other possibilities include:

• "I help people grow their own food by providing the right seedlings for the particular season and site" (tells more than "I'm a gardener").
• "I design home office layouts to maximize productivity" (tells more than "I'm an interior designer").
• "I help people get focused—I'm an optometrist."
• "Fabrics and patterns are my passion. I am a quilt artist and love to turn other people on to this wonderful art."

> **Exercise:** Take time right now to draft a self-introduction. Start with your usual generic explanation and then pare it down and spice it up. Try a number of different approaches. Inject your personality, warmth, and passion. Say it out loud until it feels comfortable, a natural expression of who you are and what you want to convey. Think of different networking situations you might be in over the next month, and consider the adaptations each might call for. Practice, practice, practice. Now you're ready when someone asks you, "What do you do?"

Be Prepared

Be prepared by anticipating the opportunities and thinking about the people you may encounter. When possible, investigate the individuals or group. I was reminded of this rule one evening when I invited the family of a friend's foreign exchange student to dinner. They were visiting from Spain, and

I was excited to have the opportunity to practice my Spanish and talk about Barcelona, a city that I love. However, I got so involved with the menu and preparations that I neglected to check in with my friend to get an update on what she had learned about the family now that she had spent a week with them.

They arrived, and we had a lovely meal. As I served dessert, I discovered that the father's consulting business was similar to mine. I felt caught off guard. I was in my hostess mode and found it hard to shift gears to thinking about how to handle this rich networking opportunity. Oh, to find some work in Barcelona! If I had known ahead of time, I would have been more prepared, confident, and resourceful in finding ways to pursue our common interests.

Be prepared to come away from an encounter with something tangible: suggestions for follow-up, an exchange of information, and phone numbers. Offer your card. You can have a calling card whether you are employed or not. I have my personal cards in addition to my business cards. It gives me great joy to see my vision in print: Earthsteward, Mediator, Peacemaker. My son has cards too: Soccer Player, Collector of "Magic: the Gathering" and Baseball Cards. You can have cards printed cheaply at your local copy center, or on your own home computer using some of the attractive precut stationery you can purchase at office supply stores.

Networking is a vital tool for social connection, business success, and balanced living. Use these opportunities to practice and polish your impromptu speaking skills. **Anticipate** (Who else might be at the library program on learning to surf the net? If I get there early, could I make a new computer-using friend?). **Clarify** (What I really need is a network of resources and people who can help me when I am confused by my computer; plus I am always looking for reliable housesitters, great takeout food, and a job for my teenage daughter this summer). **Customize** (The other participants will also live in this area and are also new to the Web). **Consider the Context** (This is a free, public class and the focus is on learning).

You are ready to think on your feet, introduce yourself with enthusiasm, and initiate new contacts!

GO TO MEETINGS TO SPEAK AND BE HEARD

Some situations call for thinking on your feet even when you don't take the initiative. For example, you're attending a meeting or gathering, and someone asks you a question or draws you into the discussion. The best preparation for any meeting you sit in on is to assume you will have an opportunity to speak. Otherwise, why are you attending? Study the agenda carefully in advance. If there is no printed agenda, call the convener and ask what is planned. Find out who else will be there and think about any agendas they may have, especially hidden agendas. Plan the ideas you would like to contribute and the message you want to register with your colleagues. Bring along any figures, data, or information that may be relevant. Think about how you can fit your thoughts into the MRS. P. format you have learned.

Once you are in the meeting, think of yourself as a presenter. You're "on" as soon as you are in range of the other attendees. Remember not only to listen attentively but also to **appear** to be listening attentively. Monitor your body language—posture, expressions, and behaviors. Other participants are forming their impressions, so you want to avoid anything that would undermine your credibility and do everything to enhance it.

It is wise to initiate some remarks early in the discussion. The sooner you enter into the discussion, the easier it will be to continue to do so. Ask a question. If you find that the meeting is running poorly, take the initiative to try to turn it around.

Is there no agenda? Say: "Could we take a few minutes to clarify our agenda? It would really help me be a better participant." Is it hard to enter into the discussion because people are interrupting and not listening to each other? Try offering this suggestion: *"Could we take a few minutes to set some ground rules? I am having a hard time finding a way into the discussion."* Everyone at the meeting will benefit, and you will have a chance to practice your speaking skills.

MASTER YOUR TELEPHONE TECHNIQUE

A great deal of impromptu speaking comes with networking on the telephone. What are the special challenges of this "heard-but-not-seen" mode of communication? Your tone of voice becomes the listener's only clue to your feelings, attitudes, and level of responsiveness. Consequently, you must put energy into your voice. It is not uncommon for speakers unwittingly to deaden their voices by aiming them at the headset. Think of sending your voice *through* the telephone wire to keep an alive, unmuffled tone. (You will learn more about vocal energy and tone projection in Chapter 7.) Monitor the background noise in your environment, as it's often transmitted. Cover the receiver if you need to yell for someone in another room. Also, be careful not to eat, drink, chew gum, or smoke while talking on the phone. The sounds are offensive and your speech becomes sloppy.

Answer Graciously

How do you sound when you answer the phone? Is this how you would welcome someone at the door? Your initial words of greeting create a climate for the conversation to come. Why not make it a sunny day? We all know people who answer the phone abruptly, with a growling "hello" that conveys the message "I'm busy, what do you want from me?" If you want to expand your network of friends and colleagues, this particular tone of voice can be deadly. This tone is never advisable, but for a self-employed person it can be deadly! What if the caller were a potential client with a juicy proposal? A warm "Good morning, this is Susan Partnow" encourages the caller. You might try taping yourself occasionally so that you can tune up your telephone voice.

When your phone rings and you pick up the receiver, you make a contract to interact with whoever is at the other end of the line. Are you ready to fulfill the contract? Take a moment to **Stop, Center, Breathe,** and **Relax** before you answer the phone. This will only take one or two rings and will go a long way to ensure a quality conversation.

If someone calls and catches you at a difficult time, tell her. Otherwise, she has no way of knowing. She can't see the leaning tower of Pisa your unanswered mail has become or the wilting garden you're trying to rescue, nor can she witness your anxious glance at the clock. Set aside distractions. I know I am sunk unless I turn away from my computer screen. It calls to me, like the sirens to Ulysses, and I lose half of what my caller says. Ask her to hold for a moment if you need to find notes you made for her anticipated call. Be sure to get her permission before you put her on hold, and don't leave her hanging for more than about 30 seconds.

You may want to offer to return the call if you are feeling too distracted to be receptive. I find there are many occasions when I need to say: "I'm glad you called. I'd really like to discuss this. Let's find a time when I can offer you my full attention." It's hard for me to ignore the ring of the phone, but I am learning to let my answering machine take calls when I am not available for genuine listening.

Call When You Are Ready

What happens when you are the caller? First, recall the techniques we have learned for impromptu speaking: **Clarify** (Before you dial the number, think it through. Why do you want to make this call? This forethought will remind you to get out your calendar, dig up the newsletter, and pull the file on the garden club before you make the call). **Customize** (Picture the person you are talking to while you speak so that you feel connected to a real person, not a plastic receiver. Are there any unique connections between you and this person? Any particular challenges?). **Consider the Context** (Since you can't see what is going on at the other end of the line, it is crucial to be sensitive when you make the call. The best strategy is to ask if this is a good time. You want to make it easy for your partner, so check it out before you begin waltzing through your agenda). And do let her know your agenda right away—whether it's just to schmooze, ask about pruning your roses, or go over plans for the banquet. How can you expect her to dance without knowing the music?

Leave a Memorable Message

These days you are just as likely to be answered by an answering machine or voice-mail system as you are to speak to the party you want. How can you make the best use of these devices? By taking the opportunity to convey important information on the answering machine, you will save time and enhance communication. When you leave a message, provide as much information as possible. In the following example, consider how much time and frustration I have eliminated by leaving details instead of just my name and phone number: "Hello, this is Susan Partnow at 333 (pause) 33 (pause) 33, calling on Tuesday morning at 9:45. I am calling to confirm my attendance at the volunteer training session tomorrow. I will come early—by 8:15—and I can bring the bagels. Please let me know how many dozen to buy. You can reach me until 11 or leave a detailed message at 333 (pause) 33 (pause) 33. Thanks! I look forward to a great orientation session."

It works! When my colleague returns my call, even if she gets *my* voice mail, she can give me the information I need. We have avoided that tyrannical game of telephone tag.

If you have an answering machine, you bear a responsibility to callers who will want to leave you a message. If there is ever any chance you will receive work-related calls, you are wise to avoid long, cute, or musical prompts when soliciting a message. All but your best friends are likely to be annoyed at having to listen to a full minute of your favorite music, especially people who call you frequently. I try to encourage callers to leave a detailed message, but I keep *my* recorded message as brief as possible: "This is Susan Partnow with Partnow Communication Workshops. I will be returning calls this afternoon. Please leave your full name, the date, and time of your call, along with the reason for calling with as much detail as appropriate. Give me the best time and number for me to reach you, and I'll get back to you quickly. Please say your phone number slowly so I'll be sure to get it right. You will have one minute for your message." (Stating the length helps the caller customize her message to you.)

Everyday situations present opportunities for developing your skills in impromptu speaking and networking. Whether you are at a social mixer, a training class, a meeting, or on the phone, you can improve your effectiveness by forecasting and formulating. What's your forecast for the week to come? What opportunities await you? What messages and impressions do you want to convey? Begin to formulate and mentally rehearse now. You can practice the unexpected.

Part II

Making the Journey—Entering Public Speaking

A ROAD MAP FOR ORGANIZING FORMAL PRESENTATIONS

Follow these easy methods to ensure your presentations succeed with clear-cut organization.

Everything should be made as simple as possible, but not simpler.
—ALBERT EINSTEIN

Remember that imagined phone call inviting you to speak about a pet project? Accept it! You are ready to speak up when called upon. You can build on the same tools you've learned for managing nervousness and impromptu situations and extend them to guide you through more formal speaking opportunities. Once you accept the invitation to speak, you may begin to wonder: "But what will I talk about? What will I say?" Relax. There are some clear-cut steps to follow that will ensure that your content is relevant, effective, and interesting to the listener. In this chapter we will look at strategies for those more formal presentations that are geared to inform. In subsequent chapters we'll explore ways to manage questions that come from the audience (Chapter 5), and we'll develop more advanced techniques of persuasion and inspiration (Chapter 6).

REFLECT BEFORE FORMULATING: DESIGN A ROAD MAP

What is the first step in preparing for a presentation? It does not involve writing or researching the content, though that's typically your first impulse. Rather, the first step involves reflection about the audience, your goals, and the context, just as we learned for managing impromptu speaking. In other words, forecast before formulating. Design a road map before you set out so that you know where to go and how to get there. Clear thinking at this preliminary stage will help you avoid time-consuming detours and wrong turns when you approach your resources. Be ready with a clear route and destination before you face the freeway of overwhelming resources and data you are likely to find in this age of information.

Set your compass for this journey according to three essential WHY questions:

1. Why do you want to give this talk? What do you want listeners to walk away with? (Clarify **your** objectives)

2. Why does this audience want to hear it? How will it impact them? (Customize to **their** needs)

3. Why is this presentation taking place? (Consider the **context**)

The answers to these key questions provide the road map for selecting and organizing your content.

Identify Your Objectives

Why did you accept this opportunity to speak? This crucial consideration is often overlooked. People tend to accept invitations without reflection because they feel obligated or honored, or even from a sense of guilt. Those impulses may or may not be appropriate. It is essential to question and reflect carefully before you go any further if you are to meet your needs and those of the people who invited you to speak. Here are the in-depth questions to ponder:

• Why do you want to give this talk? Will it meet some personal agenda items—fulfillment of certain goals, career advancement, relationship building?

• Why you and not someone else? Is the topic appropriate for you? Do you have the needed experience or knowledge?

• What will your purpose be in making this presentation? What are the outcomes you will seek? Do you want to persuade, sell, teach, share information, entertain, motivate, build trust?

• Is an oral presentation the best way to meet this need?

Tailor to the Audience

Next you need to focus on the listeners. Without them there would be no reason to talk. Find ways to tailor to their needs and make them the central focus of all your preparation. Your listeners come with their own assumptions, expectations, needs, and interests.

• Who is in the audience? How diverse or homogeneous a group is it?

• Why will they attend?

• What is their relationship to you? To the topic?

• What is the benefit of your objectives to the listeners?

• Is this the right presentation for them? Will relevant decision makers be present?

• What is the audience's attitude toward this subject?

• What is their background, knowledge, and experience in this subject?

• What possible obstacles might you face before this audience? Is the subject controversial? Is the audience apathetic, or antagonistic?

You may need to do some research to answer many of these questions. Spend time gathering as much information as you can about your audience. It's worth it. You will prevent unnecessary side trips and backtracking down the road. The best resource is the person requesting the presentation. Meet with her to discuss these questions thoroughly. If she is not sure, find other resources. Talk to previous speakers, call other staff or group members, send out a questionnaire. If your talk is part of a series, attend an earlier session. The time spent in this research will ensure a smooth journey later and guide development of the content. The more information you gather about your audience, the better you can tailor your preparations to their needs.

What about those occasions when it is not possible to know much about the audience? What if you are giving a talk that is open to the public at the library where anyone and everyone may attend? In such cases you might have to wait until just before your talk begins to assess listener needs by simply asking such questions as "How many of you have experience with this topic? How many of you are excited about it? How many of you have fears and doubts?"

Consider the Context

Context is the third important consideration. The setting, time, and situation are instructive in predicting opportunities to accommodate the mood and energy level of your audience. For example, if you are the first speaker in a day's series of events, your audience will be fresh. You can crank up the pace and pack more in. On the other hand, if you are the last speaker of the day, you will need to offer less information and invite more participation. End early and you will really be a hit.

To make the most of the context, ask these questions:

• What is the occasion for this presentation? Who is the sponsor?

• Is your presentation part of a larger program? What else is on the agenda? Who are the other speakers (both before and after your presentation)?

• Is this meeting one of a series? What have been the strengths and weaknesses, successes and failures of the other sessions?

• What time of the day and week is your presentation scheduled?

• Where is your presentation? Setting and location? Level of formality?

• What is the size of the audience?

If your advance investigation shows that your program is part of a monthly series, you can review the whole year's program and contact the other speakers to shape your talk most effectively. When you refer to nuggets from previous months' sessions, the audience will feel complimented and suitably impressed by your preparation and concern.

Can you see how these three questions guide you to take a unique approach to your topic according to the specific occasion? Even when you give many presentations on a given topic, forecasting before you formulate will take you along a different route for each visit. Let's consider an example.

After some cajoling and coaching, a friend of mine agreed to speak out about the adult literacy program she passionately supports. At first she planned to use the canned slide show provided by the center, but as we talked and explored the upcoming sessions, she gained confidence and created her own more personalized approach. The first presentation was on a weeknight at the local library in the neighborhood, where many potential clients who could benefit from the program resided. For this session, Judith's objective was to encourage listeners to sign up for the program. She realized that the audience would be anxious and possibly embarrassed. So she included inspiring success stories and testimonials about the dignity and comfort of study at the center. The second session was at the main downtown branch, scheduled for a weekday lunch hour. Here she realized her audience would be business people and college students who might be unaware of the extent of the literacy problem in the adult population. Her objective was to increase understanding of the challenge of literacy and to attract support, including donations of time, money, and books. She decided to explain the program from the perspective of the tutors, and included moving stories about devoted volunteers and the satisfaction they gained as they witnessed the fruits of their instruction. Judith was delighted with the responsiveness of her audiences. She was surprised to find it quite easy to select relevant stories from her experiences and weave them in, once she was clear about her objectives and the audience's needs.

Remember to take all three factors into account—clarify **your** objectives, customize to **their** needs, and consider the **context**—as you decide on a direction. They are the points on your compass. With these points clearly set, you are ready to begin gathering and organizing information.

GATHER RESOURCES

As soon as you know you have a presentation coming up, set up a folder in which to toss quotations, articles, cartoons, and drawings. Write down any brainstorm ideas or images, clip them to relevant articles, and place them in the folder. They'll act like seeds in a compost bin, germinating in the dark. When you look through the folder later—after you have developed your goals and objectives as well as your understanding of the audience—you'll be able to sort through it and toss the "weeds" while harvesting the viable plants.

Brainstorm everything your listeners need to know to achieve your journey's mission. Consider all the questions they may raise. Write each key idea on a separate card so that you can easily rearrange the sequence. Keep your itinerary defined (your goals and their needs) as you begin to identify the routes. At first, allow yourself to brainstorm freely. All ideas are good ideas at this stage.

As the time draws nearer, and you are ready to begin organizing, you will need to be more selective. Then you will ask whether each key idea helps you stay on course and achieve your journey's mission. By eliminating some of the data that is not strictly relevant to the destination, you will avoid side trips, however scenic they seem.

You may need to conduct further research to provide data, testimony, examples, evidence, and illustrations for each key idea. Aim to dispel doubts and dissolve suspicions, but don't feel compelled to produce a watertight case. Plan to keep your remarks simple and direct. Make it easy for your listeners, and for yourself.

Make Facts Come Alive

Collect humorous and human-interest anecdotes on your topic. The use of vivid analogies and metaphors transforms numbers and makes information interesting, understandable, and memorable. Consider the difference in the following statements:

(**Hard to remember**) Studies show that poverty is widespread in the U.S. and increasing. Approximately 14,961,000 children, which is 22% of all children, are living at or below the poverty level.

(**Easy to remember**) Picture the twenty houses on your block. If you imagine that they represent all the homes of our nation, you will find that the children in five of them will go to bed hungry tonight. Now multiply this by three million blocks of houses. That's how widespread poverty has become.

We can understand information only in terms of what we have experienced. Translate facts by relating them to what your listeners know. Here are two more examples:

Vague fact: We use a lot of water in the USA.
Vivid illustration: A single flush of the toilet uses more water in 5 seconds than the average family in Africa uses all day.
Vague fact: It's dangerous to sneeze while you are driving.
Vivid illustration: If you sneeze at 55 mph you will travel 250 yards with your eyes closed.

You will significantly enhance your presentation by turning the hard data uncovered by your research into vivid, human-interest illustrations like these examples.

MAXIMIZE ATTENTION AND RETENTION

Our ability to tune in and retain information is imperfect. We use only about 15 percent of our brain to process what we hear. What do we do with the other 85 percent? We daydream, worry, fantasize, and plan for the future. Even immediately after hearing a brief presentation, the average listener remembers only half of what was said. After a few days, recall drops to 20 percent. Retention doubles when visual aids are used and improves even more when audience participation is included in a presentation. (More will be said on the use of visual aids and audience participation in Chapter 9.)

Given these facts about the average person's attention span, the wise speaker develops strategies for helping her listeners remember what she says. Here are seven tactics that you can incorporate into the content of your presentation:

1. **Establish a pattern:** The more associations that you build into the material, the more you can mitigate the forgetting.

2. **Keep it simple:** Most of what you say will be forgotten, so be highly selective of the information you choose to present, and reinforce your points often.

3. **Build in variety and balance:** Where you place each bit of information within the presentation and how you present it affects the way it is remembered.

4. **Motivate your listeners:** Give them compelling reasons to believe that the subject at hand is important to them.

5. **Prepare a strong opening:** If you gain their attention right from the start, you will be on the road to maximum retention.

6. **End on a firm note:** Be sure you leave your listeners with a clear message to remember.

7. **Use Vivid Language:** Your audience will remember distinctive and colorful words and phrases longer.

Let's look at these seven strategies more closely.

Establish a Pattern

As humans, we naturally seek a pattern in everything we see and hear. We look for similarity, closure, symmetry, and categories to provide recognizable and comforting patterns in order to accommodate new information. The mind also has a strong need for orientation in space and time. Having these patterns is like having the proper software for creating a database. We can't enter any data until the template is formatted. Have you ever been confused by a speaker who never established a frame of reference for her topic, so that you could not fathom the organization or construction? At such times, the ability to receive and understand information is blocked until something happens to create a pattern and it all clicks into place. Your job as a speaker is to foster the "click" so that it occurs as quickly as possible.

Listeners hear what they expect to hear, so the more you orient them towards your ultimate goal, the better they will be able to receive your message. The power of suggestion influences perception. Remember how the world suddenly became filled with sports cars or vans as soon as you began shopping for your last car? Or full of babies as soon as you found out your sister was pregnant? This means that the road map you are designing for your presentation needs "sign-posts" along the route, including key words, headings, previews of what is to come, and frequent review.

Your listeners will begin gathering and recording data efficiently once you establish the categories that define your presentation. Each time you transition to a new subject, recapitulate what you have said up to that point, using key words you want them to remember, and then show the connection your previous remarks have to the next topic. Looking back and then forward allows your listeners to form an outline in their minds that is as clear as the one in your notes.

Different types of information fit into different patterns. Here are some typical patterns that people find natural and easy to follow:

• **Chronological order:** for information that can logically be laid out in a sequence (in 1970 . . . then in 1980; first, second, third; past, present, future; infants, toddlers, school-age kids, teens)

• **Spatial order:** geographic, physical, political, or sectional subjects (villages, towns, cities; U.S.–Mexico–Canada; top, middle, bottom; outdoors, indoors)

• **Functional or topical:** for information that can be grouped according to qualities, aspects, classes, types (legislative, executive, judicial; logging industry, forest management, environmental regulations)

• **Question-answer or problem-solution:** a persuasive approach for introducing change, offering new ideas, recommending actions, or getting approval (**problem:** traffic; **cause:** too many single occupancy vehicles; **solution:** increase carpool lanes)

• **Comparison or analogy:** describes one activity or quality in comparison to another (current vs. past year; adult vs. child learning style; groups go through development stages the same way children do)

The use of a pattern will help the listener—and you—follow along and retain more of the information. It doesn't matter which pattern you choose. It is the explicit, dynamic use of any pattern that improves retention.

Again, at each natural transition in your outline, review how you arrived at that point. Unlike the reader of the written word, the listener of the spoken word does not have the chance to look back for a missed point if her attention wanders or confusion sets in. Like the creators of excellent radio programming, you need to find ways to accommodate new listeners when they tune in to the middle of your presentation. Even those whose attention remains constant will find the brief reviews reassuring.

Keep It Simple!

An oral presentation is not the appropriate forum for relating masses of information or detail. A talk introduces the essential elements of a subject and cultivates attitudes, enthusiasm, and impressions. Offer some factual information as illustration and support, but supply the details or technical information in a handout. The classic studies by the psychologist George

Miller revealed that humans can retain only a maximum of seven or, more likely, five items that are conveyed orally. He calls this the magic number 7, plus or minus 2, for short-term memory. You can make your talks most effective if you limit yourself to five—or even three—key ideas.

Help the audience with your information by grouping details into identifiable chunks. We do this automatically when trying to remember a series of numbers. For example 3267848737 is easier to process as 326–784–8737. This "chunking" process enables listeners to optimize their ability to process and retain information.

Limit the *length* of your talk as well as the amount of information you convey. Even preachers have adapted to the shortened attention spans of the late twentieth century. A century ago sermons often went on for more than two hours. Nowadays preachers know that the pews will start to empty after a quarter of an hour. More than 80 percent of students report that 20 to 30 minutes is the maximum length of time they can listen to a lecture before their attention starts to wander. A serious, in-depth speech rarely needs to exceed 15 to 20 minutes. An award acceptance speech need last only 3 to 5 minutes, and a sales talk up to 10 minutes. Be sure to create breathing space between ideas, by using repetition, examples, and anecdotes.

Build in Variety and Balance

Dynamic design of your content is critical to sustaining attention, as well as the dynamic delivery we will discuss in later chapters. Why is this so? The human mind automatically tunes in to novel stimuli, and filters out what is familiar. Your listeners are responding to a new topic and a new speaker at the beginning of your talk, which raises their level of attention. But it soon begins to wane as you, your voice, and the material become familiar. What can you do about this phenomenon? Find ways to recapture interest by building in new "beginnings" as you progress through your talk. For each main point, develop a strong opening and a preview to prepare the listener for the journey ahead. Spice things up! Use a visual aid or an anecdote; vary the activity; change the pace every five minutes or so. Make generous use of questions. They are powerful stimulants, arousing interest and involving your listener.

People learn and become motivated in different ways. Some individuals require tangible details and specific examples along with a step-by-step explanation. Others need a sense of the larger picture or vision before they can take in any details. Analytic types crave data, hard facts, and statistics; listeners who are more motivated by emotion and appeals to the heart prefer anecdotes and personal experiences. To appeal to all learning types, offer stories and examples for the visionaries in the group, as well as facts to back up your assertions. If you provide variety and balance for each of your main ideas, they will be digestible to a wide range of listeners.

Motivate Your Listeners

As you plan your content, bear in mind these additional factors that will help you arouse and motivate your listeners:

• **Shared interests:** You will best capture listeners' attention by tailoring the topic and content to their interests, as we have seen. Make your mutual interests explicit. Point out any commonalities, joint history, relationships, and experiences. Demonstrate to the listeners how your topic impacts on them from their perspective.

• **Identification with the speaker:** How the audience members respond to you as an individual will determine how well you can draw them in. In addition to building rapport through naming shared interests, work to minimize your differences by removing any distractions and handling any uneasiness. (We'll explore the impact of attire in Chapter 8.) Listeners respond to speakers in stereotypical ways. The "isms" will abound—sexism, ageism, racism, classism, lookism. How can you anticipate and build on the assumptions the audience is likely to make? For example, if you are a young person addressing a predominantly older audience, consider saying the following: "You may be thinking I look young enough to be your granddaughter. And perhaps I am. But I have already spent over ten years perfecting these canning techniques. I look forward to sharing experiences with you so we can find even better ways to preserve healthy, delicious food." By minimizing the listeners' potential resistance to you, you will enhance their receptivity to the topic.

  • **Setting the mood:** As the speaker, you set the climate. Remember to express your positive regard for the topic, for the audience, and for the occasion. Smile and be enthusiastic. If you're not glad to be there, the audience certainly won't be. Start with a personal anecdote that shows what triggered your interest. Let your pleasure and enthusiasm shine through. (We'll explore how to use your voice to foster enthusiasm in Chapters 8 and 9.)

  • **Feelings of safety, comfort, and security:** Tend to the audience's physical needs, establish rapport, and create a comfortable emotional environment. Attention and receptivity diminish if the listener feels uncomfortable, preoccupied, or upset. Consider the energy level of the audience. Provide a 10-minute break each hour, and keep attention and energy high by breaking longer talks down into several shorter talks. If possible and appropriate, have people stand up and move around. Your audience will be as grateful as passengers are on long car trips when you stop for a stretch. Help prepare the listener for the demands your talk will place on her. Forecast the length, breadth, and complexity of your talk so that the listeners can steer their attention and listening skills: "In the next 20 minutes . . . We will practice . . . There will be time for questions. . . ." Use clear signposts all along.

• **Opportunity for self-expression, activity, and social interaction:** Sitting in an audience enforces passivity, shuts down responsiveness, and diminishes arousal. This makes it hard to sustain attention. Build in opportunities for them to participate. For longer talks, provide a change of pace by offering brief break-out sessions during which people can discuss among themselves what they have heard. Such opportunities for interaction dramatically raise the energy level in the room. (Look for more ideas on interaction in Chapters 5 and 9.)

With these suggestions in mind, watch the audience members continuously, and edit accordingly. Are they interested and engaged or bored and restless? Surprised? Pleased? Annoyed? Do they show understanding or confusion? Shorten, expand, clarify, eliminate, and reorganize content in response to your observations. Observe the behaviors of the audience—body language and facial expressions—especially eyebrows and mouth. Are they yawning? Smiling or frowning? Are their eyes lifeless and faces fixed? Or is there a watchful silence with lively and alert eyes, heads nodding and bodies leaning forward? Be ready to modify what you say in response to this feedback. The more you plan to use your prepared talk as a road map rather than a set script, the more you will be able to respond to your audience. The adaptations generated by your careful observations demonstrate your thoughtful interest in the audience. They will reciprocate with thoughtful interest in your topic.

Prepare a Strong Opening

Take full advantage of the high level of audience attention and retention at the outset by beginning with a carefully designed opening. A strong start will also help build your confidence and poise. Let's review the critical tasks to accomplish in the opening of your talk:

- Gain and hold attention
- Establish rapport
- Build credibility and gain confidence
- Hook the listeners' interest and prepare them for your talk
- Address the audience's unspoken questions: What's this talk about? Who are you? Why are you the speaker? Why should we listen to *you* talk about *this?* How will it benefit us?
- Set the ground rules for handling questions

If you will be introduced by someone, ask her to tell the audience about your credentials and background as well as the topic. Meet with her in advance to guide her. (More on this at the end of this chapter.) Respond and build on that introduction once the floor is turned over to you. Be sure to weave in any extraordinary events of the moment, such as unexpected weather or major news stories. Then bridge to your strong opening. Have fun. Get creative. Take time to craft an opening that you feel excited about. This first paragraph, along with the ending, is often the only part of a talk that I memorize.

Here are some ways to open your presentation:

- **Share a common experience:** "When I was a girl, my dream was to dance in Swan Lake. I may not be on pointe, but I am thrilled to be here to help you, the finest dancers in the Northwest."
- **Offer a startling or curious statement or statistic:** "Some of us have bigger houses, bigger bank accounts, or bigger debts. But we all have exactly the same amount of our most precious asset: time."
- **Ask a question (usually rhetorical):** "Would you be

willing to spend the next five minutes finding out how to help bring peace and healing to this planet?"

• **Elicit involvement**: "Raise your hand if you ever feel nervous when asked to speak to a large audience."

• **Present a mystery opener**: "When you fold your arms, which is on top: your left arm or your right?"

• **Offer a compliment**: "It is an honor for me to address an organization that has earned the respect and trust of people not just throughout the state but all over the country."

• **Use a quotable quote**: "As Eleanor Roosevelt once said, 'You wouldn't worry so much about what other people thought if you realized how seldom they do.' "

• **Tell a story**: "There was a speaker who traveled to Wenatchee to address the Rotary Club's annual formal banquet. Her suitcase was sent on to Walla Walla. She gave the speech in her sweats."

• **Paint a mental picture or guide a visualization**: "Imagine this: You're on the bank of a steep cliff on a warm spring afternoon. The wind carries the scent of apple blossoms. You hear the squeal of children at play."

• **Share something personal**: "The first time I was called up to a stage to speak, I tripped on the stairs and shredded my stockings. I quickly stepped behind the podium so I could hide my skinned knees. I've been bluffing boldly ever since."

Notice that I have not suggested telling a joke. Humor is a wonderful ingredient for your presentation, but it may be best to leave joke telling to the professional comedians. It's too easy for a joke to go flat or even offend some listeners. Use your natural sense of humor to share personal stories of irony and life's foibles.

Exercise: Using each of the suggested opening styles above, create your own examples of strong openings that you might use in a given presentation.

End on a Firm Note

The ending of a talk offers another tremendous opportunity to reinforce your message. Listeners are likely to retain what they hear last. Take advantage of this knowledge by explicitly signaling the coming of the conclusion to reengage their attention, and then make the conclusion forceful, definite, and memorable. Never end with a shrug or meek "I guess that's all," or a nondescript "Thank you," or a self-effacing "What I really meant to say was . . ." Leave on an upbeat, rousing, or inspiring note when appropriate.

The following are some helpful hints for ending your presentation:

- **Summarize or review** the main points in somewhat different language, but don't add new information.
- **Make it dramatic:** Use quotes, proverbs, or anecdotes; refer to popular songs or movies.
- **Revisit the techniques used in your opening:** This approach neatly frames your talk like a set of matching bookends.
- **Leave the listeners with a clear message of what you want them to do:** Express hope, and suggest specific actions.
- **Build in a transition** to what comes next, especially if yours is one of a series of presentations.

Use Vivid Language

The journey is at hand. You have clarified your goals, selected varied and exciting examples and anecdotes, established a clear pattern, and crafted strong openings and endings. Now it's time to put it all together and try it out by talking it through, out loud. Since written language is different from the spoken word, it is crucial to talk the presentation through to discover how it will work for the listener's ear and your tongue. Remember that in speech, sentences are shorter, simpler, and more direct. Rhythm and inflection are vital.

If you feel a need for a written version of the talk, your language will be fresher if you tape-record yourself and create the transcript from the spoken word. Vary the length of sentences. Build in snappy phrases, slogans, labels. Try using a recurring phrase. I remember using this technique when I arrived in the train station in Washington, D.C., on a Citizens' Train of grassroots lobbyists from the Northwest. We were greeted by our congressional representatives. I was thrilled to have the opportunity to speak for our group. I structured my comments this way: "Are you listening, Congressman Lowry? We've come to ask you. . . ." "Are you listening, Congressman Foley? We've come to tell you. . . ." "Are you listening, Senator Evans? We've come to remind you. . . ." In my conclusion, I exhorted, "We are the grassroots. Are you listening? We must be heard."

Use language that paints pictures and invites involvement. Remember that unused 85 percent of the listener's brain? Fill it with sights, sounds, movement, and feelings that relate to your mission. Involve your listeners. Create some mystery. Create a pattern of dots that their minds will connect.

Keep it lively, flexible, in the moment. Avoid feeling wedded to a script. Most speakers find that the best way to maintain freshness is to use notes only for key words and phrases, rather than for complete sentences. (See Chapter 8 for suggestions on rehearsal and Chapter 9 for managing your notes.)

PUT IT ALL TOGETHER

When I have a presentation to prepare, I use the worksheet below as a road map. I fill out the first part very early in my preparations, to help guide my research. I use the table as a barebones outline for the body of ideas in the initial organizing and developing of my game plan. Think about an upcoming presentation and try filling in this worksheet as an outline for your ideas. Feel free to include more than three objectives or three main ideas, but keep the research about limited retention in mind, and resist going beyond five or six.

W O R K S H E E T

TOPIC:

OBJECTIVES: (*Clarify*) What do I want to happen as a result of this talk? What do I want listeners to learn, feel, and believe? What is my personal agenda? What does my audience need?

1.
2.
3.

AUDIENCE PROFILE: (*Customize*)

Knowledge of subject?

Level of skill?

Attitude toward subject?

Motivation for listening?

Advantages of subject?

Disadvantages?

Relationship to organization?

Age, sex?

EVENT: *(Context)* What is the setting and time? The program's purpose and agenda? Are there other speakers?

OPENING: (Draft a paragraph that will arouse interest and establish credibility and rapport.)

BODY: (How will you transition between your main ideas? What is the approach you will take? How might you use data, visual aids, interaction?)

MAIN IDEAS	ROAD MAP: (transitions/structure)	"SPICE": (exercises, visuals, anecdotes)
1.		
2.		
3.		
4.		
5.		

CLOSING: (Leave a lasting impression; reinforce the message; end on an inspiring, challenging, positive note.)

MAKE INTRODUCTIONS CAPTIVATING

Introducing a speaker offers an exciting opportunity to begin developing your confidence and skill as a presenter. Like a talented warm-up band for the main act at a concert, a successful introduction helps pave the way to a successful presentation. The road map for this short excursion takes you along the same route as for a full-scale presentation. In other words, even for a two-minute introduction, you must tailor to the audience, focus on your objective, open strongly, and end firmly. And you have to do it all with special sizzle.

After you accept the challenge to introduce the topic and the main speaker, ask yourself first, "What is the objective of this introduction?" It is almost certainly meant to prime the audience, to evoke interest in the topic, and convey confidence in the speaker. You will need to persuade the audience that the topic is relevant, important, possibly even urgent for them. Inspire their admiration for the speaker by offering the degrees, experience, and expertise she brings to this topic. But avoid, if possible, reading a résumé or going through a boring chronology. Instead of a laundry list, offer a testimonial. The most effective introductions include a personal anecdote that connects the audience to the speaker vicariously through your relationship, and thus builds trust and rapport.

Your time in the limelight as introducer is brief but contains all the elements of a full-blown presentation. Keep it short—one or two minutes, three at the maximum. The example below is well under 200 words and takes slightly more than one minute to deliver:

The event is an informal gathering where the participants are on a first-name basis with one another. The guests are about to enjoy a performance that portrays eight famous women. If you were the introducer, you would look once at Elaine as you begin; then keep your eye on the audience.

TASK	TEXT
Arouse with a strong opening.	Elaine Partnow received the vision for *The Quotable Woman* one dark night as she lay abed during troubled times almost 20 years ago. She had decided to give up her 15-year career as an actor, and she was deeply grieving her mother's sudden death. Lying in the gloom, a light suddenly appeared to her. She was amazed to find a clear image within the light: It was a book. Elaine told me she could see the cover, the title, the layout of the pages, the contents, everything. It was spooky, as if she could actually thumb through the pages.
Make it personal to connect with the audience (in this case, women).	
Establish credibility and credentials.	In the light of day, she conducted a library search and discovered that existing collections of quotations included very few selections by women, and there was no volume devoted exclusively to women. So Elaine began a sojourn that would lead her—after 18 years of research into the world of women's history—to create five editions of the book that has become a classic reference of quotations by women.
End strongly with an inspiring call to action.	Elaine believes the vision of *The Quotable Woman* was a last gift, left to her by her mother. We are fortunate to share in that gift today, as Elaine joins her acting skill to the selected words of eight remarkable individuals. We are delighted to present "Living History Portraits of Great Women." Let's welcome this talented artist. Elaine?
You begin applauding and continue to do so while Elaine approaches.	

When *you* are the speaker being introduced, instead of putting yourself at the mercy of your introducer's talent and preparation—or lack thereof—provide her with a couple of paragraphs tailored to the occasion. She will be grateful, and you will guarantee that your audience is well informed and prepared for your talk. Include some anecdotal information, credentials, experience, and any honors or awards that are relevant. Be selective and keep it lively. Don't be shy. Show how your topic is relevant to the audience and why you are suited to be the presenter.

Sometimes there is no one available to introduce you. In this case, weave the key elements of an introduction into your opening remarks. Clarify the topic and explain how it will benefit the listeners. Mention your relevant training, experience, or credentials related to this topic. Name any previous contacts or personal connections to the sponsoring group or event. Most important, express your pleasure at having this opportunity.

With this road map for organizing your talk, accompanied by the techniques you learned in Chapter 2 for managing nervousness and Chapter 3 for impromptu situations, you are ready to present yourself effectively in a variety of settings.

FIELDING QUESTIONS AND MANAGING DISCUSSIONS

Learn the skills to manage free-flowing situations and transforms traps into opportunities.

. . . they give of lungs a vast expense,
But little passion, thought, or eloquence
—CONSTANTIA GRIERSON,
EIGHTEENTH-CENTURY IRISH POET

When you make a presentation, the audience will appreciate an opportunity to ask questions. Welcome these question/answer sessions as opportunities for participation and interaction, and you will transform your fear of confrontation. Indeed, keep in mind that these interchanges offer proof that your audience is listening, involved, and interested. Here is the listener's chance to communicate with you. Here is your chance to uncover and fill any gaps in your presentation, emphasize certain ideas, and clear up misunderstandings.

HANDLING QUESTION/ANSWER AND DISCUSSION SESSIONS

What are the cornerstones of a successful question and answer session?

• Respond to questioners and satisfy their needs.
• Hold the interests of the larger audience uppermost in your mind.
• Keep the session safe and comfortable. Be graciously assertive.

To make sure you maintain control of the question/answer session, it is essential that you proceed as you do for all successful journeys: Plan and prepare in advance. Even the most polished and experienced presenters spend considerable time being briefed on how to handle likely questions. Follow their example and invest the time to brainstorm a list of objections, issues, and questions that might come up. Do this well before the actual date of your presentation so that you will have the opportunity to do whatever preparation seems appropriate to master related information. Imagine the really hard questions. Invite your most argumentative friends and colleagues to challenge you. Then practice, practice, practice.

Let your audience know how you will handle questions. Can they ask at any time? At the end of each section? Or should they reserve all questions for the end? It can take a brief transition to get the discussion period warmed up and going. When you call for a question, prepare the way by pausing. Wait, and show with your body that you are sincere, rather than quickly moving along as you say, "Any questions? Well, then . . ." It takes the listener time to switch gears from her passive listener role to an active questioner role of formulating and responding. If questions are not forthcoming, you can call on people directly, especially if they have approached you at a break and you've gotten their permission. "Tyler, you had an interesting question at the break." Or plant a question by arranging for a friend to ask the first one. Another strategy is for you to pose the first question yourself: "Something that frequently comes up . . ." "At the last meeting a participant asked . . ." "You may be wondering . . ." Once the discussion session gets going, it's often as though the dam has burst and the stream of inquiries and reactions begins to flow.

Successfully managing questions requires that you listen carefully. You can only provide satisfaction to your questioner when you hear and understand what she is asking. Yet it is easy to allow preoccupations and negative self-talk to distract you while under the pressure of the moment. Review and practice all of the mental preparation techniques described in Chapter 2. Be ready to *Stop, Center, Breathe,* and *Relax* throughout your question/answer sessions. Visualize yourself staying focused and attentive to the questioner while she forms her inquiry. Notice her nonverbal as well as verbal message.

It is often wise to repeat or rephrase a question. This confirms your understanding of it, helps others in the audience hear the question, and provides you more time to formulate your response. Ask for clarification or amplification if appropriate. (Note that asking for clarification can also buy you more time to reflect and formulate.) Take your time. Breathe. Keep your ultimate objective in giving the talk clearly in mind as you begin to formulate. Follow the MRS. P. approach introduced in Chapter 3, and be succinct.

The process is straightforward, yet anxiety about handling these free-form question and answer sessions is prevalent and intense. Do any of the following common fears seem familiar to you?

• I'll have to answer questions and get into subjects I'd rather not cover.
• I'll lose control of the situation and people will become confrontational.
• They'll ask me something I can't answer and I'll lose my credibility.

There are ways to handle each of these concerns. We will review a number of strategies. The key is to remember that *you* are in the driver's seat—not the questioner!

Don't React; Respond

Every comment and question deserves a response. Yet too often we feel controlled by the questioner and limited by the question, and we react defensively. We feel as though we're back in the classroom, needing to please the teacher and get a good grade for giving the "right" answer. Left-over feelings from little-girl days lurk beneath our grown woman's appearance and make us long to gain approval, rather than to control the process or to innovate. So we squeeze and stretch and push and pull all of our ideas and information to try to fit into what we perceive the questioner is asking.

But in the case of your presentation, *you* are in charge of the journey. You own the map, and you can steer the course. You can even alter the route. Instead of fitting your thoughts into the form of the questioner's inquiry, you can "get a better question" and adapt the inquiry to your agenda.

Get a Better Question

Some questions are unclear, irrelevant to your purpose, negative in tone, or too narrow or personal to be of interest to the broader audience. In such cases, it is essential to get a better question in order to create a bridge to your agenda. You can get a better question by adding on to what was said, thus rerouting, broadening or narrowing the original question. You can answer with a question or ask for specifics. At all times, keep your road map handy. Remember to relate everything to **your objectives** and the **audience's needs.** Route each of your responses accordingly.

Imagine that you're at a PTA meeting where you are seeking parent support for the auction that will raise the money to bring in an artist-in-residence. Your objectives are to gain support for arts in education and to elicit help from the audience to run the auction. The audience needs what is best for their children. Someone asks, "Why doesn't the PTA support an after-school band?" Here are some ways you could manage this challenge:

• "I'm glad you have raised this issue of a music program. As I have mentioned, arts education is a vital tool for enhancing our children's commitment to learning and for encouraging positive after-school activities. If we work hard together we can raise enough money to bring this artist to our school and begin to work towards introducing other fine programs, such as music."

• "You raise an important issue about the lack of a music program. I share your frustration at the inadequate funding for arts in education. And that is why I need the help of everyone in this room to help make this worthwhile program happen."

• "There is a question about the PTA's priorities in how we spend the money we raise. Unfortunately, cutbacks in funding have hit a number of our school's programs, including the band, chess club, and tennis team, as well as the artist-in-residence initiative. I invite you to attend our board meetings where we set priorities and make hard choices about all of these outstanding programs. Most importantly, I urge everyone to work together to pass the next bond issue to restore the funds."

If the question is overly long or confusing, try to restate it simply and ask for confirmation. This restatement also affords an opportunity to reframe the question in a manner more suited to your purposes. Address only those aspects you find most relevant, rather than trying to answer every part of a multiple question. Imagine the questioner saying, "Well at the school my daughter attended last year they had so many special programs that the teachers felt they never got to teach the basics, and the PTA was able to raise a lot of money for these programs because they got a local business to lend one of their executives. Have you considered these issues?" You could respond, "Let me make sure I understand your question. You are asking how we are working with our teachers to insure that the artist-in-residence program enhances the curriculum. And, second, you are suggesting that we seek support from the business community. Am I correct? Thank you for bringing up these vital points. The PTA is in full agreement, and we have worked closely with our head teacher to select a program that directly ties into the classroom language arts and science programs. I would love to talk to you at the break to learn more about how to gain business support for our program."

Don't feel compelled to answer every nuance when someone poses a series of questions. Focus on the main point, especially as it pertains to your agenda. Remember that the questioner deserves a response but you are in control of the subject matter.

Maintain Grace under Fire

Notice the common elements in all of the examples above. The questioner is never criticized or put down, no matter what her tone or intent. Instead, she is validated and assumed to mean well. Even if you suspect otherwise, it is always wise to treat the question as legitimate and well intentioned, and to address the questioner as a partner, not an opponent. Avoid pointing out areas of disagreement or irrelevancy. Rather, give emphasis to areas of agreement and common ground. You remain firmly and respectfully in control.

These behaviors send a clear message to the participants that it is safe and desirable to ask questions, raise issues, and get involved. Whether at the dinner table, a board meeting, or the podium, the listeners will remain awake to your message. Eliminate red-flag words that put the questioner down. Abolish alienating phrases, such as "you people." Remember that no matter what words you use, if your body language or tone of voice expresses sarcasm, defensiveness, condescension, impatience, or animosity, the members of the audience will clam up, and you will lose the opportunity to find out what is on their minds.

What if someone in the audience becomes disruptive? First, be assured that it is extremely rare and unlikely that you will be confronted with someone who wants deliberately to scuttle your presentation. But in case you are confronted with such a person, and to help you not worry about the possibility, here are a few suggestions:

• The group will hold you in high regard when you are able to maintain grace under fire. Indeed, if hecklers or obnoxious individuals act out, the group will often actively help you suppress those undesirable behaviors.

• If some outburst occurs while you are the speaker or moderator, pause to acknowledge the interruption. Then, while making eye contact with the heckler, continue your talk. This action will send a strong signal that you are not going to get hooked into the game. If the heckler speaks again, you need to respond more directly. Again, pause and look at the person and this time say, for example, "I will be happy to speak with you at the break, so please come down here. Right now I am going to continue with the agenda as planned."

• If, under the most extreme and unusual of circumstances, the person persists, stop and get help from the host or event coordinator and have the individual removed from the group. Do not continue speaking or allow the heckler to continue to distract you. Do not engage in arguing with the heckler. Resist the temptation to respond in an insulting tone.

• Most importantly, don't take any outburst personally. The troublesome individual would probably harass anyone who was in your position. Thus it is the role or position you represent that she resents, not you yourself. Or, more likely, she has a problem independent of you. Manage the situation firmly and kindly, and the group will be grateful, relieved, and filled with admiration.

Fortunately, these situations are much rarer than our fearful fantasies would have us believe. I must say, in all the years I have spent as a speaker and workshop facilitator, I have rarely encountered such challenging behaviors and have never faced a heckler. In everyday speaking encounters, it is unlikely you will meet unruly situations, but you can expect a few tough questions.

Deflect Hostile Questions

If, in any question/answer session, you feel as though someone is challenging you in a way that is hostile or competitive, you might take to heart some lessons from aikido, the martial art of defense. Unlike karate, where you use *your* concentrated energy to deflect an attack, with aikido, you use the attacker's energy to transform an attack into an opportunity. Never react or push back. If someone challenges you in a hostile way, transform her energy, welcome her emotion, and go in the same direction rather than away from her. You might say, for example, "I, too, feel a great deal of passion around this issue." "I'm glad you raise these serious concerns." "Let's look at what it is that arouses such heated tension."

It is vital to remain gracious *and* assertive. Breathe deeply. Do not take it personally. Mentally convert a challenging "why" question into an inquiring "how." Keep your voice firm and pleasant. Resist judging the person. Ignore insinuations, such as "You women," or "Dearie, when I was your age . . ." Disregard these jabs. Take pride in remaining calm, gracious, mature, and focused on your objectives.

When people behave with hostility, they are reacting emotionally. Their thought processes are shut down. Often you can defuse these situations by asking for more information to reengage their more reasoned side. Their replies will inevitably be more reasoned than their initial strike:

- Would you please repeat your question?
- Before I answer, would you please say more about your views?
- What leads you to object to this?

It is often helpful to identify the feelings behind the questioner's hostile remarks: "I hear your anger and disappointment that your son has quit playing the trumpet now that the ensemble has disbanded." By rephrasing the question you can transform the tone. Compare the questioner's underlying message when she says, "You're just trying to raise our taxes for foolish frivolity. Don't you people know it's the 3R's we should fund?!" Your reasoned rephrasing: "There's a concern about the educational value of arts education." Try that verbal aikido and *use* their attacking energy instead of resisting or fighting it: "I share your concern and that is why I put so much effort into reviewing the studies that evaluate the educational benefits of the arts. It is indeed the substantial and well documented improvement in the 3R's that arts education yields that brings me to this project."

Planning and preparation will help you anticipate some of the objections listeners may have to your presentation. Then you can seize the initiative and handle possible objections by bringing them up in your opening remarks or during your presentation. That way you prevent the need for them to be raised later. Of course, the challenge here is to avoid raising concerns that people wouldn't have thought of otherwise.

Certainly, if you discover that you have been mistaken, be ready to admit it graciously, and then move on. Your credibility will only increase. "Thank you for pointing that out." "I will add that to my report."

Honesty, Still the Best Policy

One of our worries may come true. Someone may ask something that you don't know. Rest assured, there are lots of ways to say "I don't know" yet preserve your credibility. The only response that is sure to destroy it is one that is a bluff and built on illusion or falsity. Recall the wise words of Calvin Coolidge: "I have never been hurt by anything I didn't say." Here are some phrases and approaches you can use with integrity:

- "I want to make sure I get the latest figures. I will call you tomorrow."
- "That's an interesting question. What do others in the group think?"
- "Julie, you have dealt with this issue. Would you share some of your experiences?" (Only defer to someone who will be comfortable and capable.)
- "I don't have information on that program, but I can find out and send it to you later."
- "We have a task force that is researching this very issue. They will be ready to report next month."

As long as you are sure of what you know and what you don't know—and are clear where to set that boundary—you can handle these probing questions effectively.

Bridge to Your Agenda

The Cajun people have a wonderful word for good fortune. They call it a *lagniappe* (lan-yap). The wise manager of discussions is always alert for a *lagniappe within each remark.*

That is why you want to "get a better question." You want to find a way to bridge every question to your agenda. Begin to think of each question as an opportunity to reinforce your message—even the hostile questions. For example, consider taking this next step when answering the angry father: "I hear your anger and disappointment that your son has quit playing the trumpet now that the ensemble has disbanded. *I am angry too. In fact that's why I agreed to chair this auction. I hope you will join me in the struggle to raise funds for arts education.*" The father's anger becomes an opportunity to recruit him as an activist.

Even the "I don't know" response can become an opportunity: "I don't know why the band has been dissolved. But I will look into it. Perhaps you would join me. *Let's all of us attend the next Board of Education meeting and find out what we can do to restore funding. Let's demonstrate the priority we give to arts in education.*"

Let's consider an example at the hotline volunteer training session where your agenda is to encourage people's confidence so that they will make the commitment to staff the phones. A participant asks, "How can you possibly keep up-to-date on all the resources you need to refer callers to?" You respond to her concern: "We have just installed a wonderful new on-line service that is linked to the county referral data base. All you need to do is click on a few key words and the program searches for the most appropriate referrals." And you go on to add your important message: "*Our top priority as an agency is providing you, our volunteers, with full support. I can assure you that you will have the resources and help you need to feel equipped to help our clients.*"

Notice the *lagniappe* in italics. Here was the opportunity to add encouragement to the potential volunteers. Another opportunity might come at the PTA auction meeting when a parent asks, "Are there special forms we should use for donations?" You reply: "We have a whole packet of materials to help make our solicitations go easier. The kit includes a fact sheet on the program, a sample script of things to say, a list of ideas for possible donations, and a donation description form for the donor to complete." Now you continue, to add a lagniappe: *"If each of us gathers just three donations, our auction will meet our goal and we'll be able to schedule the first artist-in-residence by the first of the month. Please pick up three of these kits before you leave tonight."*

Manage the Session like a Gracious Hostess

Managing a question/answer session calls for you to combine the skills of a hostess with those of a chairperson. You want everyone to feel comfortable and important and you want to stick to the business at hand.

Balancing the concerns of the individual questioner with the comfort of the audience as a whole can be done through nonverbal communication, as well as by maintaining control of the content of questions and answers. Offer eye contact to the questioner while you listen attentively to her query and while you initiate your response. Then turn your body and gaze to include the audience as a whole as you bridge into the essence of your message. You may glance again at the questioner, to show that you have her needs in mind, but avoid making this an exclusive one-on-one conversation. Indeed, if the questioner was hostile, do not look back once you turn from her. This deliberate turning away while giving the question a respectful answer will help discourage continued retorts.

If there are a lot of questioners, you need to take on the role of a traffic cop. Who will be recognized? How long will each questioner be allowed to talk? Will everyone get a turn? How can you be fair in choosing who to call on? These are concerns that preoccupy the audience and can cause tension in the room. It is up to you to manage the flow carefully so that audience members can devote their attention to the discussion. One way to create a queue is by naming the people in the order you see their raised hands: "Joyce, then DeeDee, and then Tyler." In order to make sure the discussion isn't monopolized by the overzealous few, you will want to draw out the shy members.

Monitor the audience's attention span and keep each of your responses brief and focused. Keep track of your allotted time so that you remain within established limits of your program. Provide for overflow if you can't get to all questions. Can you talk to them at the break? Give them your E-mail address or phone number? Manage your time so that you end with the presentation under your firm control. A common problem occurs when the presenter loses track of time and allows the group to thin out and trickle away, and finally ends weakly by shrugging her shoulders and commenting, "Well, I guess that's all." Let the participants know you are about to end. Tell them you will field one last question. Then, as you come to the close of the question/answer period, you can bridge one last time to your agenda so that you end with a strong restatement of your message-conclusion. Remember, the last thing said is the first thing remembered.

TAKE THE PANEL CHALLENGE

What an honor and a challenge to participate in a panel! You will want it to be successful for everyone involved, so work closely with the conveners, but don't assume they have the expertise and experience you need. Ask a lot of questions to ensure adequate preparation. Make sure you understand the purpose of the panel, the role for each participant, and the context of the situation. Also, learn all you can about the other panelists. If possible, call each one several weeks before the event to talk about your respective topics and approaches. Checking in with the other panelists will help you plan your own remarks and enhance your effectiveness in managing the impromptu questions and the discussion among panelists.

Remember to look and act like an esteemed guest even while the other panelists are speaking. Listen attentively and look alert. Check your posture, eye contact, and facial expression. Weave comments made by the other panelists into your remarks. Follow up their remarks with observations of your own.

If you are the moderator of the panel, you have several additional challenges. You must answer for yourself the key questions: "What is the purpose of the panel, the role for each participant, and the context of the situation?" Then you want to communicate the answers to each participant. Inform them of their time limits as well. Tell the panelists about the other participants and suggest that they prepare questions for each other.

Your role will be to introduce the panel as a whole in terms of its theme and goal and then to introduce each panelist. You can make your job easier by asking each panelist to supply an introduction beforehand. You will also need to provide transitions as the spotlight shifts from one participant to another. Plan your remarks ahead of time, but be prepared to listen carefully and weave comments about the actual presentations into your transitions. Another vital task for the convener is to compose the summation. Plan a strong conclusion to close the discussion and open up the question/answer period. But remain flexible and ready to alter your remarks according to the topics and issues that emerge during the actual panel discussion. Your job throughout will be to monitor the time, balance participation among all members, and facilitate the process. Think of yourself as that gracious hostess, working to make all of your guests comfortable—the panelists and the audience.

Begin the discussion period by encouraging the panelists to engage each other. Then throw it open to the audience. During the question/answer period, assist in directing each question to the appropriate panelist and perhaps to a second panelist for follow-up, especially if you anticipate a different perspective. Toward the end of the allotted time, signal to the panelists and the audience that the next two or three questions will have to be the last. Finally, after taking those questions, bridge to your summation and end the entire event firmly, with a considerate word of acknowledgment and thanks to all the participants. Incorporate elements of the discussion, and restate the essential message or theme of the panel.

FACILITATE ORDERLY AND PRODUCTIVE GROUP DISCUSSIONS

Our world seems to be run by teams and committees. With more of us in the workplace, and with citizen groups growing in every neighborhood, it is likely that most of us will need to facilitate a discussion from time to time. How do you prepare for a group discussion? You can apply the same approach we have used for impromptu and formal presentations:

- **Anticipate:** What questions and issues are likely to be raised? What information and resources will you need to have available? Will all key players be present?
- **Clarify:** What is the purpose of this meeting? What do you want the group to do? Is the focus on content or relationship building? Is it primarily for decision making, brainstorming, problem solving, training, or strictly information giving?
- **Customize:** Who will attend and how do the issues affect

various participants? What is their involvement and commitment?

• **Consider the Context:** What will the general climate be? Are people looking forward to this discussion or have they been forced to attend?

Ideally you can review the purpose and agenda with participants ahead of time. If not, make the first item of discussion a review and adjustment of the agenda. Next, clarify everyone's role. When you are the facilitator, it is your job to monitor the group to prevent anyone from monopolizing the discussion, to ensure that everyone has access to the floor, and to keep the climate safe and respectful. You also have to keep track of the time and agenda to ensure that you stay on track. That's a lot for just one person to undertake! It is often advisable to divide these roles among several individuals: one to facilitate the interaction, another to chair and track the agenda, another to record, and yet another to be the timekeeper.

The role of facilitator and chair is different from that of the presenter. Rather than inject your own ideas, you elicit those of the group. Indeed, it is advisable for the facilitator to resist giving her opinion, because it might bias the group and inhibit healthy disagreement.

Group discussion extends the methods we've learned for good conversation. Like conversation, it depends on everyone contributing, taking turns, sharing ideas and information, listening, and being tactful and sensitive. But rather than seeking pleasure, as in conversation, group discussions aim for the crystallization of thought. They help the group keep the larger intention in mind: to integrate each person's best thinking into the whole, not to push through one person's opinion over another's. Remind participants that they each need to offer thoughtful input, not glib empty words. Each needs to remain open to listening and hearing in order to reach consensus, to learn from one another, rather than stick to firm, preset positions. Unlike a debate, where you want to exploit the opponent's weaknesses, in a discussion you want to foster collaboration, respect, sharing, and listening.

Quality listening during a discussion is a great challenge and must be a highly active process, involving questioning for clarification, paraphrasing, and even note taking. Set aside distractions, pay attention, and look attentive. Work hard to keep your mind open and suspend judgment. Listen for the key ideas; then relate the facts and examples to those key ideas. Focus on *what* is being said, not how it is being said or by whom. And resist a natural tendency to be swayed by the vocal and visual impacts. Be a critical thinker about ideas and information. Ask yourself the motive or purpose behind any one person's remarks; probe for what is missing or weak, and seek what makes each comment significant.

Watch for fuzzy thinking, overgeneralization, and false analogy. Distinguish between opinion and knowledge. As the chair, it's important for you to clarify the question to be discussed, with terms understood and agreed upon by the group. Help different factions listen and be heard. Direct discussion towards solutions that are constructive, positive, and useful, as opposed to those that are judging, blaming, or even theorizing and generalizing.

Help the group move towards action. You may need to break a very large issue into smaller elements for discussion. Be prepared to propose different methods, such as brainstorming or diagraming, and periodically to summarize points reached, agreements made, the next item to discuss. Ensure that the conclusion is not reached prematurely, and that it is clearly stated and understood by all. Prevent anyone from monopolizing the discussion; enforce courtesy and respect for all. Translate emotional language into more neutral terms.

Establish ground rules for the discussion at the very beginning. When will you take questions? What are the rules of courtesy you will observe? What is the time frame? Elicit agreement on explicit ground rules and the discussion will proceed much more smoothly. When the group is diverse in terms of gender, culture, personality style, power, and position, these rules become vital to ensure fair play and equitable participation. Adjust the amount of time you devote to the development of ground rules according to how long the group has been meeting and the sensitivity of the topic. For a minor topic, you can unilaterally propose a few simple ground rules and cover them in just a minute or two. For an ongoing group or a substantive and controversial topic, it is worth taking considerable energy and time (probably 10 percent of the group's total time) to collaboratively develop a set of rules.

Mutual agreement upon a set of ground rules makes it much easier to manage any difficult behaviors. You can use the rules to keep the situation under control: "Dr. Laura, we have agreed to take turns and listen to each other. Could you please hold your remarks until Emmy finishes?" "Those are interesting observations, Newt, but we have established a different agenda for tonight."

If the situation requires firmer intervention, use *I*-statements that emanate from yourself and provide a direct statement about what is causing the problem. Avoid judgments or assumptions about motives or intentions. The *I*-message has three parts. Begin with a neutral, objective description of the problem: "There are a lot of side conversations going on. . . ." Next, express the effect the behavior has on you or the group: "This distracts members of the group." Then express what you want to change: "So please either share your thoughts with the whole group or save the conversation for the break."

Try a range of techniques to increase participation. A group size of 8 to 12 works best for participation and discussion. If the group is large, arrange time for small break-outs into pairs, trios, or clusters of 5 to 6 people to discuss various issues on the agenda. Then you can check in with the groups and ask them to report to the group as a whole. This arrangement mirrors our representative democratic system and allows everyone to participate. Another technique is the round-robin, during which you structure the response pattern so that each person in the circle takes a turn responding. These techniques create a safer space for many otherwise reserved participants.

Recognize Gender Issues in Group Discussions

Discussion leaders must be vigilant to prevent a gender imbalance among participants. In the last few years much attention has been paid to the ways men and women communicate, and linguists generally agree that there are identifiable differences in style that sometimes make understanding between men and women difficult. When it comes to group discussions, the wise facilitator will study the different tools men and women employ within a discussion. Many of the rules in the dance of conversation are influenced by gender, especially the rules that govern who chooses the topic and turn-taking. In general, it has been noted that women follow rules of facilitation, whereas men follow rules of competition.

What are the rules of facilitation?

• Promote dialogue: two-way conversation in which each speaker is understood.
• Ask questions.
• Reflect feelings.
• Encourage the other to continue.
• Expand and elaborate upon existing topics.

What are the rules of competition?

- Interrupt and dominate.
- Seize the floor and monopolize it.
- Control the topic.
- Refuse to talk on someone else's topic.
- Withhold information.

Note that neither of these strategies for discussion is inherently better or worse than the other. Most men are perfectly comfortable with the masculine style of speaking, and find the feminine style frustrating and circuitous. Women, on the other hand, feel at ease with the feminine style, and are often intimidated in mixed groups. So there is no call to judge, here, only to understand what is happening when the two styles clash in a group discussion *you* are facilitating.

When a woman actively facilitates a conversation, she usually seeks first to understand her partner fully, with the expectation that her turn will come to be understood. She believes that her partner will eventually switch to the facilitative role and ask her about her own perspective without the need for any direct request. It is unusual for a woman to disappoint another in this expectation. Alas, the trade is more rare in mixed company. More commonly, a man will bask in the airtime created by a woman's artful facilitation, and his rules do not include any need for taking turns. According to his rules, the other participants in the group, male or female, will seize the floor if they want it. He means nothing personal by dominating the conversation, and he will not take it personally if others interrupt.

For most women, a lifetime of conditioning makes it hard to gain control of the floor unless their partners or other members of the group offer to yield. Interrupting is simply not an option. The notion that politely waiting for a turn will be rewarded is deeply ingrained. Study after study shows that in mixed gender groups, men account for almost all of the inter-

ruptions. Women tend to follow these interruptions with silence, giving indirect consent to the change of topic. Men, on
the other hand, will follow interruptions with more interruptions, which can make a discussion between men seem parallel, rather than integrated.

In group discussions these issues translate into important
political considerations. If women *wait* for their turn, and men
take their turn, then women do not get heard. Further, though
men are quick to accuse women of talking too much, in fact,
during a typical conversation, women curtail the length of
their contributions when they do make them, reflecting their
urge to keep the sharing of the floor equal. So once we do finally manage to get the floor, we hurry through our turn as if
to say, "What I have to offer isn't any more important than anyone else, so why take up airtime."

Of course, not all men display the assertive, interactive style
described here. Many men with a more passive, considered
style are also shut out of discussions by interruptions and free-
for-alls designed to control the floor and topic. Likewise, we all
know women who are adept at dominating discussions. But
with power, influence, and control all up for grabs in a discussion, anyone relying on the typical feminine style will lose out.
Since all participants in a group ultimately lose if they don't
hear from everyone, group leaders are wise to establish ground
rules that address the problem. If you are the leader of a group,
you must structure the discussion so that everyone gets a clear
chance to speak. You can be sure that left unstructured, the
discussion will be dominated by the masculine style of speaking, whether coming from a man or a woman.

Remember that gender issues in group dynamics are not
just a matter of the frequency with which people speak but
also the content of what they say. Some women are very talk-
ative and manage to interject, contributing mainly affirmations of what others have said. When it comes to offering their

own comments or shifting the topic, however, they back down or are drowned out. Calling for a round-robin, where each participant in turn is asked to contribute for a specified time, can help ensure that every voice is heard. To encourage expression of all thoughts, especially those that may differ from remarks by someone of higher status, ask participants to take a few moments for silent reflection and note taking before beginning the round-robin. By setting clear rules for the discussion, you can help men become better listeners and help women learn to assert themselves appropriately by telling interrupters to back off.

If we are to be effective facilitators of group discussions, we must ask ourselves how much we have been influenced by conditioning that makes it hard for us to stake our own claims in a mixed group. What personal work do we need to do to overcome the difficulties we might face in this regard? First, we need to affirm the feminine style of conversation as valid and good. It is good to give and take. It is good to listen as well as to contribute. As women we can also continue to honor our preference for equal empowerment, while at the same time asserting that what we have to say is important. We *can* interject ourselves into discussions, speak up, and resist the impulse to hold back or hurry through our remarks. We *can* stop raising our hands, waiting to be recognized, and seize our turn. We *can* hold off interruptions by continuing to talk through overlaps, gesturing, or saying plainly, "Please let me finish." When courage fails, consider Helen Keller's counsel, "Avoiding danger is not safer in the long run than outright exposure." Or, in the words of Sister Elizabeth Kenny, "It's better to be a lion for a day than a sheep all your life."

If you have been given the role of facilitator in a group situation, then you have a mandate to be sure people stay on the topic. While you may have to step on someone's toes to prevent a derailment, you can trust that most people will appreciate your assertiveness in this regard. The problem of red herrings in discussions is often a gender issue. Studies show that in mixed-sex conversation, men generally want to control the topic, and they usually do. Although women may offer a large variety of viable topics, theirs are typically ignored by both the men and the other women in the group. If you are a woman leading a discussion among both men and women, be aware of this predilection towards control, and prepare in advance how you will keep the group on task. Be as firm as you need to be.

When is a discussion resolved? Here, too, we see a strong gender contrast. Since men more often use discussion to resolve or fix things, once it's over it's over. Their conversations are like a tennis game, ending in a win, a loss, or a draw. You can't play the same match again. For women, however, since we more often use speech to express ourselves rather than to reach a conclusion, there is always time to circle around again and revisit the conversation to discover further nuances, deeper shades. Aha! This is why, when I reintroduce a subject of concern, my husband so often objects, "But we already discussed that!" As facilitator, be aware that men often feel frustrated by the feminine style of circling back, and women often feel cut off when men want to get to a clear resolution and move on. Just knowing that tension can arise because of these different styles will help you diffuse it. You are the ultimate timekeeper. You can say to a woman, "I'm afraid we have to go on to our next agenda item," without making her feel that she is repeating what the group has already heard. And you can say to a man who expresses impatience, "I think we have ten more minutes before we have to move on to the next topic," reassuring him that you *will* move on.

Remember that we always generalize when we talk about gender traits. Don't be surprised if a man won't let a topic go and a woman shows impatience to move on. But do be aware that you can diffuse tension based on differences in style.

USE INTERVIEWS TO TALK YOUR WAY TO GREATER OPPORTUNITIES

Whether you are hoping to join a board, considering a teaching position in your church, or looking for a job, performing well in an interview presents a great challenge. How do you get ready? As suggested for other types of question/answer sessions, the key is to prepare, prepare, prepare, then practice, practice, practice. Use all of the mental training techniques: breathe, positive self-talk, affirm, visualize, mentally rehearse. Anticipate the questions that are likely to be posed, such as "What are your strengths and weaknesses? How would you handle this problem? What would you do if this happened?" Recruit a friend and role-play the interview situation. Practice taking your time in order to think before you answer. Use the MRS. P. formula presented in Chapter 3 to organize your thoughts; remember to breathe; and feel free to "get a better question."

Study your past experiences and résumé carefully, and make sure you include every talent and success your prospective associates will appreciate. Think of specific examples to back up each skill. If you are being interviewed to join the board of the new theater that is forming, don't just say you enjoy marketing. Tell them how you helped double the membership of the garden club you belonged to, taking it from a membership of 100 to 200 in a single year, by developing a marketing campaign using a newsletter.

Apply the lagniappe technique to each question. In an interview, the lagniappe is always a translation of "See—I'm the one for you—Choose me." Let's say you are applying for the role of volunteer coordinator of the Parks Department's new

Sunday morning program for seniors. The question is, "Do you have any experience with computers?" You answer with some of the specifics *plus* how they relate to the job you seek: "I have done a great deal of word processing and desktop publishing, and I have also used some databases." You continue so that you can add your lagniappe: "*I especially enjoy creating attractive flyers and newsletters and have edited and produced these for my temple, which has a membership of 1200. I noticed your system has Microsoft Works and Microsoft Publisher. I know how to use these and do a mail merge to send flyers about upcoming events in an efficient and timely fashion. This could be an important way to increase participation in this program for seniors.*"

Be ready with a positive self-introduction. You can bet that one of their first questions will be some version of "Tell me about yourself." I allowed myself to be thrown by this a few years ago when I went to meet with a big outplacement firm to explore how I might provide presentation skills coaching to the executives they were trying to place. I was expecting a focused discussion on the specifics of my approach to coaching. Instead, they treated the meeting like a job interview and began with a very open-ended "So tell us about where you came from." The question felt so unexpected and wide open that I felt my whole life story flash before me. Fortunately, I quickly came to my senses and realized they really didn't care about my hip days as an L.A. teenager, my political awakening in Berkeley during the 1960s, or my sophisticated adventures in Paris. I chose times and episodes that illustrated the breadth of experience I could bring to coaching executives—my training as a speech therapist, my experience as a clinic director, and my experience giving workshops in public speaking skills.

It is important to avoid raising any negative concerns. Avoid negative comments and resist airing any dirty laundry. Watch how you handle questions about your failures, conflicts, frequent committee changes. Turn your answers into positives: "I took the initiative to leave the board when I realized a reorganization was inevitable within the next six months." "I spent the first few years living in this area exploring different congregations. Now I know that this is where I belong." "I am looking for a transfer because there is no room for advancement in my present department." Avoid getting hooked by such questions as "Don't you get along with your supervisor?" "Wouldn't it be tough to attend evening meetings when you have young children?"

Before you go to an important interview, study the chapters on voice and delivery very carefully (Chapters 7 and 8). Your nonverbal behaviors will be observed closely. It is essential to make a strong initial impression. You want everything—the way you dress, your posture, your body language, and your voice—to project a strong message of poise and confidence.

Another important lesson for interviews is to recall that they are not one-way conversations. You, too, want to learn about your partner in the interview. Cultivate your questioning skills. Seek out the organization's particular needs so that you can demonstrate your ability to fill them. Your thoughtful preparation reflects well on your knowledge and initiative: "What are the board's top priorities for next year?" "How is your program affected by the increase in catalog sales?" "How did parents respond to your library campaign?" Also, prepare ahead for what you wish to learn, such as start date, travel requirements, time commitment, opportunities for training, supervision, evaluation, decision date, and the method for notifying you.

Close the interview with a summary of what you have to offer and a direct question about how they see your chances. Review the three most important things you want them to remember about you, and thank them for the interview: "I appreciate this opportunity to speak with you today. You have a wonderful organization and an exciting opportunity for the right person. I think I am a good fit for what you need. As we've discussed, I have skill and confidence with the computer, I enjoy working with seniors and have a good rapport with them, and I can take the initiative and use my marketing experience to build this program. From what you have learned so far, do you think I am the right candidate for this position? What else could help you be comfortable in selecting me?"

With this forethought, your confidence and ability to respond will help you stand out as an exceptional candidate.

TAME THE MEDIA

Andy Warhol once said, "In the future everyone will be world-famous for 15 minutes." Life in the late 1990s seems to bear this out. We all may face an opportunity to promote our message through the media, whether in our private, philanthropic, or professional life. You never know when a reporter may stop you on your way out of a meeting to solicit your perspective. Ask around and you will be amazed to find out how many of your neighbors, friends, and relatives have been interviewed for TV, radio, or a newspaper.

I have often volunteered to be the spokesperson for organizations I belong to since, as you may have guessed, I enjoy the challenge. In the beginning, I noticed how compelled I felt to drop everything at a moment's notice as soon as a reporter called. Perhaps they wanted to record a statement via telephone for their radio program. (They are always working on a tight deadline, of course.) Eventually I learned to negotiate for some time to prepare—and the quality of my responses vastly improved. No matter how tight the deadline, I found I could always carve out a few minutes: "I'd be delighted to give you that statement. Let me just take a few minutes to gather my notes and screen out interruptions. Can I call you back in 15 minutes?" Then I would quickly run through the road map of my goals, their needs, the context, and fit this into the MRS. P. format. I would choose the three key points I wanted to get across, if that was all I could say (and it usually is)—and come up with an interesting hook and anecdote or example for each.

It is easy to forget that reporters have a very different agenda from ours. Their concern is other than to promote our cause, educate the public, or even tell the whole story. At best they see themselves as watchdogs for the public at large. Often they seek to exploit and even sensationalize the news to tell an interesting story. They are drawn to the sparks of controversy rather than to balanced reason, crisis rather than stability, and conflict rather than cooperation. In any case, they are not public relations agents for your case or organization. You have to find a way to frame your message in a way that can make a good story. Sprinkle your talk with those 7- to 15-second pithy gems the press can so readily use. They want information, images, and quotes they can't get elsewhere. They are often working on several stories under tight deadlines. They will appreciate a press packet that provides them with background information. They'll probe with questions to find out who stands to gain or lose, what ramifications there might be, what information you can confirm or refute.

TV presents the greatest challenge, as they will select a mere 20-second sound bite to use from that satisfying 10-minute interview, and their selection will be determined in great part by what constitutes the most potent visual image. At the holiday season each year, I used to help run a Boycott War Toys campaign, to educate parents about how violent playthings increase aggressive behavior in children. We would display positive creative playthings—such as art supplies, dress-up costumes, and sports equipment—alongside a display of such really offensive items as toy planes bearing nuclear warheads and realistic-looking bazookas. I was very excited that the TV stations came down to our event and I patiently answered every question they asked. We soon learned what a mistake we had made when we watched the interview on the 6 o'clock news. The worst war toys were glamorously displayed, along with a voice-over statement I had offered about how popular these war toys were and how parents felt pressured to buy them because their children begged for them. No mention of the studies that showed their impact on increasing conflict and hitting! No image of the preferred gift possibilities!

The lesson I learned was to provide *only* those images you want displayed. Talk *only* about what you want your message to say. Package your words in short bite sizes. Sidestep the questions that lead you where you don't want to go. I also learned to be a much more critical viewer of the nightly news, as I began to appreciate how the story of each person or group might be similarly distorted by what was edited out.

If you are invited to a talk show, make sure you tune in and sample the moderator's style before you show up. I naively assumed that I would be a welcomed guest on a local TV talk show, since they had sought my participation. I showed up filled with good feelings and enthusiasm about my worthy cause and notes full of information, studies, and statistics—and little else. I was caught very much off-guard when—on live TV—the moderator began her interview with a hostile tone and challenging question, "Why make such a big deal about toys? We all played with guns when we were kids and we're not shooting anyone." I survived, but it felt terrible and my effectiveness was hampered. I hadn't yet learned the Aikido of conflict and verbal sparring. Now I'm ready to take her on! Learn from my experience. Do your homework. Study the program and the moderator. And control the direction of the interview.

Make the lagniappes happen by keeping in mind at all times the three most important elements of the message you want to deliver. These elements are the valuable cargo or treasure chest that make this trip worthwhile. Unload your treasured message early on and repeat it whenever possible. Don't wait for the media to ask the right question. Start with your most precious jewel; make it the first thing you say and repeat it at least twice—you may not get to the rest of the message. If you represent a group, speak on its behalf rather than giving a personal opinion. As you do with any questioner, you have the right to ask reporters for clarification, to get more information, or to ascertain their opinion or position. Resist trying to answer a question you don't fully understand. You also have the right to be able to finish expressing your thoughts without interruption, so feel free to ask a zealous reporter to stop interrupting and let you finish.

Some journalists may try to lay a trap to get you to lose your temper or contradict yourself. Keep cool. Stay calm. Don't get defensive. Defuse highly charged questions by restating them in a more neutral tone, devoid of any disparaging words or references. Reframe a reporter's barb: "Isn't your little group a bit radical and overly sensitive about tiny plastic figures?" with a positive response: "Parents are concerned about toy figures because . . ." If she pushes further to disclaim your position, continue: "I'm glad you raised that issue because many viewers may also wonder. The truth is . . ." Just keep your tone friendly but firm so that you don't sound sulky or defensive.

Nothing is ever "off the record." Leave "no comment" for the cinema. It will alienate your viewers and send the reporters digging deeper. Don't let a reporter put words in your mouth. It is important to be confident in dealing with the media. Leave shyness and hesitancy behind. Be gracious but assertive as you correct them: "No, that's not what I said. . . . Here's what I mean. . . . That's not correct; let me tell you how I feel. . . ." If they interrupt you with many questions, try saying, "You've asked me several questions. . . ." and then go on to reply with a gem from your treasure chest. Take every opportunity to bridge to your treasure chest with such phrases as "Let me add . . ." "I'm often asked . . ." "I believe the key issue is . . ." If there is a long silence, relax. It's the interviewer's job to manage the time. Do not volunteer unnecessary information.

Remember to keep your language vivid, concise and easily understood. Project with enthusiasm. Offer facts, but use as few numbers and statistics as possible. Create word pictures and make the facts come alive. Transform the statistic that 35,000 children die needlessly every day into what UNICEF vividly presents as the silent emergency: "Imagine 100 jumbo jets crashing, each with 350 children aboard, every day."

The preparation for these encounters with the media is similar to all of the situations we have described. Anticipate the event by practicing all the possible questions you can think of—especially the tough ones. Be aware that the reporter is likely to have an agenda different from yours. You will need to have a firm grasp of your key points at all times so that you can answer every question to your advantage.

When you find yourself in the role of facilitating a discussion, fielding questions, being interviewed, or dealing with the media, remember to welcome it as an opportunity, not a trap. You are in charge; you "own" the information and the process. You can manage the dynamics and transform the questions to bridge to your agenda. Think clearly about your goals and objectives, keep them uppermost in your mind to guide your responses, and you will find success.

PERSUASION, MOTIVATION, AND INSPIRATION

Make sure your approach fulfills your purpose.

There is a vitality, a life-force, an energy,
a quickening, that is translated through
you into action. It is your business to
keep it yours clearly and directly, to keep
the channel open. You have to keep open
and aware directly to the urges that
motivate you.
—MARTHA GRAHAM

Everyday situations often call for speaking with a special twist. Activities and ceremonial events of all kinds challenge you to motivate, persuade, or inspire. In this chapter you will learn ways to go beyond simply informing your listeners based on knowledge you have gained through research or personal experience.

Do you want to persuade a board to allocate funds; motivate PTA members to volunteer; inspire colleagues to support a project? Do you want to galvanize people into action? Do you want to celebrate the life and accomplishments of a loved one? The quest is to present your message in a way that gets the results you want. These speaking engagements call for passion and a deeper understanding of the listener. When you speak at a commemoration, the challenge is to inspire your listeners to celebrate with you in the most meaningful way possible. You speak to touch your listeners' emotions and uplift them.

In the case of persuasive speaking, the results you seek frequently ask for a change of heart. You are asking the listeners to alter what they do, think, or believe. How do people usually respond to change? With resistance! Inertia, a powerful force on human behavior, is hard to overcome. People are reluctant to initiate a new behavior; they want to cling to existing habits and patterns. Persuasive speaking is the art of conquering inertia and generating the desire for action in the listeners—to get them to *do* something with the ideas you present.

MAKE A PERSUASIVE ARGUMENT

How do you feel about developing your skills of persuasion? Does it arouse fears of propaganda and devious manipulation? While persuasiveness can be misused, as can any tool or skill, you can use it in the service of a positive purpose by helping people move toward a worthwhile activity. The next time you turn on your TV, notice how most commercials are carefully crafted to appeal to our desire to do something good for ourselves and others. Auto manufacturers show us how the right car will protect our family members, improve our sex appeal, or bring prestige and admiration. You may reject the hard-sell approach in many ads, but there is much to be gained by learning the art of the "soft sell," which is meant to enlighten and educate the listener. More often than not when we speak, we are in effect selling our ideas, our opinions, or our proposals for a better world. The boundary between persuasion and manipulation is maintained by remaining honest, sincere, and forthcoming.

The soft-sell approach keeps the buyer at heart. The skillful salesperson helps the buyer identify her needs and then shows how a particular product or service meets those needs. We can do this to inspire people to action! As women, we are highly sensitive to people's needs. And giving ourselves permission to cultivate this sensitivity as a way to persuade people has tremendous potential, both for boosting our self-esteem and for getting important work done.

There are two basic approaches to persuasion:

1. **Make a direct appeal:** Tell the listener what you want up front. This approach works best in most cases. Americans

typically appreciate getting down to business without surprises or wasted time, and we don't like to feel manipulated.

2. **Begin with the problem:** If you anticipate immediate, automatic, or absolute opposition, establish the need first. Prepare the way, create receptivity, and then work up to the appeal.

With either approach, you can see how vital it is to know your audience, as we have seen for impromptu and formal presentations in earlier chapters. Follow the wisdom of Aristotle: "The fool tells me his reasons; the wise man persuades me with my own." Skillful persuasion and motivation—indeed all forms of effective communication—depend on discovering how the listener's needs and interests dovetail with your own goals.

Once you determine your approach, incorporate the elements described below into your presentation. Most of them are part of any effective presentation. They complement the "MRS. P." formula (Message, Reason, Support, Propel) developed in Chapter 3, and the more formal road map described in Chapter 4. However, you'll find that a few legs of the trip need expansion when your aim is to persuade, and there are also several new stopovers. The art of persuasion calls for care in developing your timing, your approach, and your choice of what to include or exclude. It is not unlike the careful packing you do for an exotic journey. Make your selections fit the audience's needs and your objectives at every step. Unpack the items in the order that builds your case most appropriately for the situation.

LEARN WHAT MOTIVATES PEOPLE

What are the levers that can nudge people out of their inertia? According to the renowned psychologist Abraham Maslow, unmet needs are what drive our behavior and fuel our emotions. He identified a hierarchy of needs. As we satisfy one level, we are drawn to the next through an upward spiral of motivators.

Survival is at the base of the hierarchy. Self-preservation and the satisfaction of bodily needs, such as hunger and thirst, take precedence over all other needs, and all other concerns will be ignored until they are assured. **Security** is second in Maslow's hierarchy of needs. Once people have the food they need, they seek comfort and safety.

Belonging to a group is next on Maslow's hierarchy. We need a family or clan that includes us as an integral part of a group, in which we are listened to, supported, and accepted, indeed loved. Next on the hierarchy comes **self-esteem.** We naturally seek prestige within the group. Our ego craves respect, recognition, and status, and it urges us to be ambitious and to take pride in our accomplishments.

At the top of Maslow's hierarchy is **self-actualization.** When all other needs are met, we can begin to seek ways of fulfilling our potential, which inclines us toward altruism and toward the all-important challenge of being of service.

When you are trying to persuade your listeners with the soft-sell approach, you can appeal to these basic drives in order to motivate them to action. Particularly when you ask for someone's help, you can appeal to her need to belong and to be of service. When you call for support for the local food bank, you can touch upon survival and security issues. When you invite someone to join a board, you offer to meet her need for belonging, prestige, and recognition.

Kindle the Desire for Action

Once you understand what motivates your audience, you can develop the map that will set them on the road toward concrete action. The following points along the route suggest the kind of road map you need. The examples provided with each point represent a brief presentation designed to persuade PTA members to help raise money for a resident artist by participating in an auction.

ESTABLISH GOODWILL AND GAIN ATTENTION

As a speaker, whether before a group or in a one-on-one situation, your first job is to encourage a positive attitude toward the subject and pique the listeners' interest at the same time. Provide enough background to orient listeners to the topic, and then give them an overview to help them form an outline in their minds and increase their receptivity. You may want to announce your ultimate goal in speaking at the beginning. That is, you give the listeners a preview of the action you propose. The following opening both creates a positive atmosphere and suggests the course the topic will take for the listener:

"Imagine your child's shining eyes when she gives you the lovely handmade basket she has woven with the help of artist Joyce Harvest Moon. Joyce is a visiting artist who demonstrates drumming techniques, tells Iroquois tales, and offers a craft workshop for children. Would you like your child to work with Joyce Harvest Moon? [Await nodding heads.] With your help we can raise the money to bring this talented, award-winning artist to our school."

CREATE A SENSE OF NEED

What sort of problem needs solving before you can meet the stated goal? Why does the problem exist? Go beyond facts and figures: Show how people are affected. Tailor your appeal to the motivating needs outlined above, such as comfort, security, and pride. Warn your audience that action is needed to avert a larger problem. Or create a sense of dissatisfaction that urges a change:

"How many of you are aware that funds were cut for arts in education? [Wait for their response.] How do you feel about our children not having music, drama, or drawing next year? [Wait again, and build on their response.] Funds have been cut despite research which shows that arts in education significantly improves motivation and performance in school."

OFFER YOUR IDEA OR SOLUTION

Be clear and direct when you offer a solution to the stated problem. Explain why you chose this particular road and what makes it the most direct route to success. You may want to explain how you reached this conclusion, including other ideas you thought about and discarded. You can avert protest by anticipating complications that might arise if your idea is implemented and then by suggesting ways to avoid them. Finally, present a timetable for applying your solution:

"We need to work together to find a way to replace these funds. We have held successful auctions in the past. Last year we raised $5,000 to purchase computers. This year I believe we can raise $8,000 so we can continue to support the science program *and* bring arts education to our children. Wouldn't you like to strengthen our school program in this way?"

DEMONSTRATE THE POTENTIAL FOR SATISFACTION

To be effective, you must prove that your idea will work to fill the need or solve the problem. There are three elements to this important component of your presentation:

• **Evidence:** Provide experiences, statistics, and expert opinions, or conduct a demonstration. Anticipate and meet objections. Resist telling everything you've learned, which might sound pontifical. Avoid using shaky evidence. If audience members find a piece of data that is questionable, they may discount all of your evidence.

• **Benefits:** This is the heart of persuasion. The listeners want to know "What's In It For Me?" (WII-FM is the universal radio station we are all tuned to!) Show them how your idea will help them. Tie the benefits to their pyramid of needs. Unlike the details or features of your proposal, which simply describe the solution, the benefits answer the *listener's* key concern, "What's in it for me?"

• **Action:** It is time to make an explicit request for the action you desire. Tell the audience what is needed to proceed, whether it be to volunteer for a committee, to allocate money for your project, to vote for your proposal, or simply to consider your new perspective.

"We can do it! We have an enthusiastic new auction chair who recently doubled the proceeds for another community group. We have promises from many of last year's contributors to make this auction a success. There are written materials that make soliciting easy, and you can call me or the chair any time for help. We have an even better location where there will be room for dancing, so we expect increased attendance.

"I'm excited! The auction will be fun and will help strengthen the community, as well as bring art education to our school. How many of you had a good time last year? I'm really looking forward to nibbling the delicious appetizers that local merchants have promised to donate. The money we raise will improve our children's enthusiasm for school. And Joyce Harvest Moon will provide experience with a different culture. What a gift for our children! We keep reading how diversity training is vital to success in today's world. What do you think? Does this sound great? [Await nods.] With the reinstatement of our artist-in-residence program, our school can reclaim its reputation as one of the best in our city.

"If each of us brings in just one auction item, if ten of us sign up to help on the night of the auction, and if most of us commit to attending the auction with friends and checkbooks in hand, Joyce Harvest Moon will be here next fall to spread her magic. How many of you will join me in making this happen? Can you help me out?" [Tips: Await the raising of hands. Don't rush. A pause builds impetus to respond. One raised hand is contagious to others. Call out the names of people you know when they raise their hands, and express your appreciation.]

VISUALIZE THE OUTCOME

End your persuasive talk with a visualization that projects the listeners into the future in order to intensify their motivation and elicit emotions. Use vivid imagery with all the senses (seeing, hearing, feeling, tasting, smelling) so that the audience experiences the potential for your predictions to come true. Paint a picture of the safety, pleasure, and pride that the implementation of your proposal will generate. Vividly describe the consequences if the proposal is ignored. When you close with a visualization, the emotional involvement leaves an imprint of your call to action on the listeners:

> "We are going to have fun and get great satisfaction by working together. Just picture your child next Thanksgiving when she comes home bubbling over with stories of Native American songs, legends, and history. Taste the luscious corn fritters at the schoolwide potlatch that will end the two-week residency. Feel the weave of the beautiful basket woven by your child. See it adorning your bookshelf where it's proudly displayed. What a shining memory for our school! Let's do it! Here's the sign-up sheet. Just check off whichever activity you prefer. Thank you for your help."

You will have noticed in the sample presentation above that a lot of interactivity is built in, in order to get listeners' heads nodding. Requesting responses to questions builds momentum for agreement and, ultimately, for involvement. Did you also notice that this presentation appealed to such basic needs as security, belonging, self-esteem, and self-actualization? Use this persuasive itinerary to organize your comments the next time you have a request to make in a group setting. You will be delighted with the response you elicit from your listeners, whether at your garden club when you ask for extra help with summer watering, or at the family reunion when you want your cousins to create a souvenir video for the great-grandparents. In fact, you can adapt this road map to private journeys, such as motivating your grandchild to get dressed, inspiring your housemate to put more creativity into his cooking, or persuading your partner to pick up the cleaning.

Note, finally, that in the example above there is no whining, complaining, or badgering. Despite any frustration you may feel, you must avoid expressing it at all costs. Accentuate the positive by pouring all of your passion into enthusiasm about the proposal. Remember: ultimately **you** are the message. The intensity of your feeling about the issue is of the utmost importance, along with your level of commitment. Nothing is more persuasive than putting yourself on the line. Share with the audience any actions you have planned. If you were rallying support for an auction, for example, it would be highly effective to display the items *you* plan to contribute, name the friends *you* will bring, and state your resolve to buy many items *you'll* use as gifts. Your integrity, commitment, and sincerity are vital to your credibility. There is great power in speaking from the heart.

HONOR THE MOMENT: COMMEMORATIVE SPEAKING

Someone's tagged you, and you're it. It may be your best friend's 50th birthday, the christening of your first grandchild, your boss's anniversary party, or the installation of the new president at the garden club. You're expected to make a speech. Breathe deeply. You know how to do this! Yet don't mistake the "casual few words" as too trifling to warrant thoughtful preparation.

When the invitation to speak is for a ceremonial purpose, such as a toast, a welcoming address for a delegation, or an award ceremony, the occasion calls for *inspiration* more than persuasion and motivation. Inspiration stimulates the mind or emotions to a high level of feeling or activity. There is a quality of exaltation, a lifting to a higher level that moves the mind or feelings irresistibly to respond. So the task is to stimulate the listener's energies, ideals, or reverence in an uplifting way. Make emotion part of the message, but direct it to the higher level needs—belonging, prestige and self-actualization.

The strategy for planning every great journey is the same, whether it's the trip of a lifetime, the annual vacation, a weekend getaway, or just an afternoon's outing. Begin by *clarifying* your objectives, *customizing* to the audience's needs, and *considering the context* of the situation. Then, for these personal situations, explore your heart.

Embrace the Personal

Let's consider the case of a grandchild's christening. Imagine your daughter has asked you to act as the hostess, and she wants you to speak at the gathering. What are your objectives? You want the guests to feel welcome and comfortable. Your heart tells you that you want to share your joy over your grandchild, show pride in your daughter, and express appreciation to those gathered. You want to mark this as a memorable occasion. What are the listeners' needs? Your daughter's are probably indistinguishable from yours. The guests' agenda will be similar, but they also want to have a good time since this is a social event. Could there be any complications? Is there discord with the in-laws? Discomfort or disappointment with certain traditions? As you consider the context, you must take all such circumstances into consideration in order to avoid awkwardness.

For any event, find a theme that best illustrates the person or occasion being celebrated, and develop an inspirational commentary. Make use of metaphor and analogy. You can weave in quotations, and, if you are with the appropriate audience, sprinkle your comments with humor—especially amusing stories that spring from personal experience. Relate historical events to this moment. Take time to explore your subject as fully as possible. Research the town, a place name, the history of the organization, award program, or individual, and build in the interesting or unexpected details you uncover. Here is an example that would be appropriate at the christening:

"The name Jessica means God's gift, and we welcome you, new spirit, as a precious gift indeed to our circle. You are named in honor of your grandmother, who would have treasured you beyond all riches. May you share her love of literature, her desire to learn, and her determination to live life fully."

Use an engaging vignette to create a mood or atmosphere that centers on the person or occasion. I might tell this story at the sendoff party when my daughter leaves to go to school on the opposite coast:

"As a young woman I went away to live in Switzerland, and at the time I did not know how long I would be gone. Your Auntie—my sister Elaine—came to see me off on this great adventure. It was a painful departure. In those days we didn't expect to speak by phone or keep in touch by E-mail. The distance seemed enormous. We lingered as long as we could and finally separated with a tearful good-bye at the airport gate. As I settled into my seat, the teardrops fell. When would I see my dear sister's face again? I looked up, and there she was! I had forgotten that my camera was looped around her neck. She had convinced the flight attendants to let her board and find me. We were so happy with this brief reunion that we laughed. It seemed a magical sign that though the miles would separate us, we would also be there for each other. Well, please don't leave anything behind—these days I don't think the airline would let me board the plane! But know that I will al-

ways be there for you, dear daughter, as you fly out of our family's
nest."

Invoke Inspiration

One way to inspire your audience's emotional response to the
occasion is to pose, and then answer, a question that generates
anticipation. Here is an example of this technique, created for
the presentation of an award to a departing board president of
the League of Women Voters:

"Five years ago when Sybil, the nominating chair, approached
me to join the board, I asked her, 'Why would I want to take on
yet another responsibility? What could possibly make it worth all
those meetings and phone calls in the face of my already overex-
tended daily commitments?' She said, 'Susan, you will mark your
tenure on the board as a jeweled season of your life. You couldn't
pay for the richness of the experience, the joy, and the learning
you will receive while serving under Jeanette's leadership. It will
be a treasure.' Sybil was right. I have grown rich with learning and
the joy of service beyond expectation with you as my mentor.
Please accept this pin as we honor you today. Each time you wear
it, reflect that its jewels represent the gems you have enriched us
with."

Parables and proverbs abound in many cultural traditions.
They also lend depth, interest, and inspiration to these occasions. Here's an example that the leader of a local Chamber of
Commerce could use at the opening of a new neighborhood
park:

"In Africa, the Benin people have a proverb that says, 'If a palm
tree doesn't cooperate with the ground, it won't bear fruit.' We almost starved ourselves in this struggle—neighbors and merchants—when we clashed over plans for this precious pocket of
land. But we have done well. Have you walked by the park yet on
a weekday morning? Our hard-won collective vision has allowed

our palm tree to bear many fruits. The square is lively with the clicking of tourists' cameras and their clucking over the view. It's filled with the giggles of neighborhood children, stumbling over the feet of weary shoppers resting on the hand-crafted benches our local artist created. I congratulate us all on an abundant harvest."

The use of a quotation lends the author prestige and credibility, along with the lyrical language. Here is a favorite, woven into a toast that you might use at the end-of-season pizza party for your daughter's soccer team:

"Our coach exemplifies Bess Meyerson's words: 'You've got to love people, places, ideas; you've got to live with mind, body, soul; you've got to be committed; there is no life on the sidelines.' Here's to our coach [raise your glass] for inspiring, encouraging, and guiding our daughters. Yolanda, you've taught them more than how to score points; you've galvanized them to work as a team and excel together with a cooperative spirit."

Your library, bookstore, and the Internet are teeming with resources for speakers, with quotations, quips, parables, and anecdotes there for the plucking. Be sure to seek out quotations and stories about women. We owe it to ourselves! You'll find some great references in "Further Reading and Resources" at the end of this book, including Elaine's *The New Quotable Woman.*

Nowhere is inspiration more important and appreciated than during a eulogy at a memorial service. Such occasions are generally meant to provide an outlet for attendees' intense feelings of loss. If you are called to this solemn task, take some time to recall aspects of the deceased person's life that will inspire the listeners to celebrate the life of the loved one. Here is an offering I gave at the memorial for a friend's young son:

"Nick's preschool teacher reminded me of this story from when he was just four years old. His mom and dad were, well, discussing some problems. And their voices got, well, louder, and their faces got, well, a bit redder. Nick took this all in with his big round eyes. Suddenly he jumped up. 'Just a minute,' he said. And he disappeared up the stairs. When he came back down he had in hand the 'talking stick' he had made at school. 'Here, take this, Dad,' he said. 'It will help you take turns and listen to each other.' Nick was a peacemaker. I believe even now he is hoping we will find peace in our hearts."

Relating personal stories about the one being commemorated or honored will bring every listener closer to that special individual. Offer the riches reaped and the lessons learned from knowing the beloved. I hope to share this tale when my adopted Aunt Gert celebrates her ninetieth birthday:

"You are such a treasure to me. A model and a heroine who knows how to find joy, reap wisdom, and learn endlessly from life. I have many of your poems posted on my bulletin board. One of my favorites ends with 'Let my epitaph read, "Her years were long, but she never grew old." Oh, how you live up to this, dear Gert. I have a photo posted next to this poem that brings a chuckle every time I see it. There you are at age 88, sitting on the counter in the middle of Nordstrom's, determinedly looking at the pictures of 3-D illusions in *The Magic Eye*. I remember your whoop of delight and amazement when at last their magic sprang into life for you. May my spirit learn the magic of your winter's ageless springtime joy."

Sharing funny memories provides the release of laughter for your audience. I recall one such moment, which was deeply comforting and memorable, at the memorial for global peacemaker Danaan Parry, founder of the Earthstewards Network. His wife, Jerilyn Brusseau, recounted this story:

"In the midst of our wedding vows, Danaan announced he wanted to sing a song for me. I said yes, of course, and breathed deeply to ground myself and get ready for the old sacred song I anticipated—probably something from the ancient Celtic tradition, I imagined. He looked deeply into my eyes and then belted out, 'Only youuuu, can make the world seem right. . . .' "

Did we roar! The whole audience broke up with tears and laughter as we recalled Danaan's great spirit and joy for life. And we felt so moved that the whole community joined to sing the song to Danaan as we dedicated ourselves to carry on his great work.

When you take these opportunities to honor those you love, you will be as richly rewarded as your audience. Reminiscing brings comfort and healing. Working hard to craft the words brings honor to the memories. The next time you are offered the opportunity, try it!

Adapt to the Situation

When preparing remarks for a commemoration, pay attention to the particulars of your situation so that you bring the right perspective, tone, and mix. It's like knowing what to pack according to anticipated weather and activities. In the list of words below, each pair forms a continuum. Before you even begin to formulate your remarks, decide where the upcoming occasion falls on each continuum. If the occasion is more towards the formal, solemn, intense end of the scale, your tone and content will be very different from what they would be on the informal, upbeat end of the scale.

> formal . . . . informal
> solemn . . . . upbeat
> past . . . . future
> serious . . . . humorous
> detached . . . . . . personal
> individual . . . . . . collective

historical . . . . . . visionary
intense . . . . light

For example, when honoring a retiring teacher, you might focus on the role she played in the school's past, whereas a tribute to the young, award-winning science teacher should offer a visionary picture of how her creativity and contributions will lead the students into leadership for the twenty-first century. Match your choice of words to the group.

If you are to speak outdoors, find out how good the amplification system will be, and consider the physical comfort of the listeners. You may want to keep your remarks short and punchy if it is hot, if people are sitting on the ground, or if they are hungry and eager to begin the meal. How large is the crowd? At a rally with many spectators, you need to speak in shorter phrases and provide more pauses to allow the entire crowd to absorb what you are saying. Is the audience settled in for a meaningful program at a graduation? Give them something to chew on. If the previous speaker was overly solemn, lighten up the climate. Emotions are highly contagious and easily amplified. You need to be aware of the audience's emotions and to time your remarks so that they allow for moments of laughter, spontaneous discussion among participants, or grief.

Are you getting the picture? In each situation, elaborate upon the road map provided in Chapter 4: Clarify *your purpose* and the *audience's interests* in light of the *context*, and you will be able to tailor your remarks with stunning results.

PUT YOUR BEST VOICE FORWARD

You weren't born with your voice; coaching techniques can help develop greater strength, authority, and beauty in your vocal image.

"How wonderful is the human voice!
It is indeed the organ of the soul."
—Henry Wadsworth Longfellow

It has been said that people will judge you by three things: your face, your disposition, and your voice. Indeed, Henry Wadsworth Longfellow called the human voice "the organ of the soul." Just as your personality gives people an idea of the kind of person you are, your voice creates an image that can either lend credibility to what you say or detract from your message. Remember Lina Lamont in the film *Singin' in the Rain?* This star of the silent movies could not make the transition to the "talkies" because all signs of glamour evaporated with the sound of her nasal voice, Brooklyn accent, and ungrammatical speech.

How aware are you of the vocal image you project? You wouldn't consider giving a presentation or attending a business function, let alone going to a party with friends, without first checking your appearance in the mirror. Yet do you ever check your voice? True, it takes more time and effort to improve your voice than to enhance your appearance with a new hairdo. But it can be done.

How did you come to sound the way you do? Think of the person you sound most like. Probably it's your mother or sister. My sisters and I sound so much alike that my father is often confused as to which one of us is calling on the phone. Yet our personalities and body types are not at all alike. Since the voice—its rhythms, tones, and inflections—is the result of *learned* habits and patterns, it is possible to change it. Voice coaching techniques can help you develop greater strength, authority, and beauty in your voice, all of which will enhance your vocal image.

LEARN THE ELEMENTS OF VOCAL IMAGE

Think of someone you know only by telephone. You have never seen her, yet you have formed a picture of her in your mind. What are the assumptions you have made about her age, education, personality, intelligence, ethnicity, and even her appearance, simply from the sound of her voice? Have you had the experience of finally meeting such a person and being surprised that she does not fit the image you've formed of her? What image do you think a stranger on the telephone forms of you?

Think of the voices that you admire. They probably exhibit a number of common, essential qualities:

• **They are easily understood:** The articulation is clear and crisp; the rate is flowing and easy to follow.
• **They are easily heard:** The volume is appropriate.
• **They are pleasant to listen to:** The voice quality is rich, relaxed, and expressive.
• **They are unobtrusive:** The voice complements the message without distracting from it, and it matches the messenger without provoking unusual attention.

You can enhance these elements in your voice. The first step is to become aware of the desirable traits, then examine your present voice patterns. This chapter will teach you how to cultivate the desired qualities. It is up to you to practice the techniques and integrate them into your everyday speaking.

Pick and choose among the many exercises. Not all of them will be relevant for you. The more you practice, the sooner you will find success. With patience and persistence, speaking with your optimum voice will become second nature. Then— *voilà!*—you will have a voice that others will admire.

When trying out new speech behaviors, exaggerate them at first. As you become involved in conversation, your attention to the new pattern will inevitably become less focused, and the exaggeration will be reduced. So, if you don't "start big," you will not end up "improved." It may feel funny at first, but be bold. Trust that exaggeration works. Besides, what seems exaggerated to you may appear minimal or even undetectable to the listener.

Curiously, a change in speech patterns may trigger emotional reactions that could surprise you. You need to watch for them and keep them from preventing you from changing your speech patterns. The physical act of speaking in a new way will not feel the same as the physical act of speaking in your habitual pattern. You may not "feel like yourself." Give yourself permission to feel differently. Coax yourself to create a new you, a second you, an improved you. Understand that when it "feels wrong" you are probably doing it right. When it "feels right" you are probably reverting back to your old habits.

START WITH THE BREATH

Your breath provides the foundation for your speech. You speak on a column of air as you exhale. Good breathing habits, therefore, are essential for adequate volume, projection, and durability, as well as for a voice that is easy to listen to. Many people go through life without ever considering the quality of their breathing, much less how the breath affects the voice. Shallow breathing leads to a high-pitched, reedy voice that has little resonance or volume. Shallow breathing also leaves a speaker deflated during and after a presentation. The goal in learning good habits is to learn deep breathing, which is at the same time natural and unforced.

Breathe from the Belly

Take a moment right now to notice your breath. How does it feel? Shallow or deep? Easy or restricted? What causes the air to go in? It's actually a matter of air pressure. Expanding the rib cage creates negative air pressure inside the lungs relative to the air outside your body. Air rushes into the lungs to equalize that pressure. Place your hand where you feel most of the expansion. Most people who are not practiced at breathing fully find that they lift their chests rather than expand their bellies or, more accurately, their diaphragms. But when you consciously expand your diaphragm instead of your chest, you create a much stronger column of air, which carries sound more steadily and more easily. The diaphragm is a dome-shaped muscle that forms the floor between the lungs and abdominal cavity. When it is contracted, it lowers and flattens, while the ribs lift up and out like a bucket handle, creating a large volume of empty space in the lung cavity. When you engage in upper-chest breathing, lifting the shoulders and sternum up, you work much harder for the gain of much less air volume. So the first step toward improving your voice is to learn to breathe from the diaphragm.

> **Exercise:** Start by bending over from the waist as far as you are comfortable, with arms dangling, jaw relaxed, and knees slightly bent. Notice how your breath begins at the small of your back and moves out and around your waist, expanding outward with each breath. Memorize those sensations. Now straighten up slightly with your hands clasped in front of you, as though you were a golfer about to make a putt. Again, notice how the breath seems to begin at your back, though a bit higher this time, just

above your waist. The breath expands out and around, *not up*. Again, memorize these sensations. Next straighten even further so that you are just slightly bent over from the shoulders with your head bowed and hands clasped in front of you, as if you were sniffing a bouquet of flowers. Notice that the sense of expansion out and around begins now in your midback. If the movement has begun to move upwards at all, bend over again as far as you need in order to get the expansion back to a movement of out and around. Again, memorize these sensations. Finally, straighten back to your corrected posture and see if you can recreate the feeling that the source of the breath is out and around and from the belly, not from the chest. This is optimal diaphragmatic breathing.

Stand Tall

Breathing from the upper chest reflects poor posture as well as stored tension. Stand up straight and tall. What happens to your breathing? Do you find that it becomes more natural to breathe from the belly? When your posture is correct, you have more room to expand the diaphragm. The following exercise demonstrates how closely linked posture is to breathing and, thus, to voice.

Exercise: Stand in what you consider to be your best posture. Take a mental snapshot of this position so that you can compare it to any corrections you make as you read through this exercise. Check your knees. Locking them cuts off your breath, so be sure to relax them and keep them slightly bent. Avoid arching your back. Keep your pelvis slightly tucked in a relaxed way. Take time to feel centered, with your weight balanced equally between your toes and heels. If you're not sure, try coming onto your toes a bit and then settling back onto your heels. You should now have the lower half of your body in good alignment. Now check your head. Keep your chin parallel to the ground so that the front of your neck is soft and relaxed and the back straight. Imagine yourself suspended from the ceiling on a string attached to the crown of your head, making the crown the highest point and allowing your body to lengthen all along your spine. Try to expand the space between your shoulder blades while keeping them relaxed and dropped as low as they will go. Feel yourself fill the space around you by expanding and lengthening, rather than shrinking and caving. Stand in this corrected posture in a relaxed yet alive way. Memorize the sensations from the tip of your toes to the top of your head. This awareness of the shape of your body and the life within it is called a kinesthetic experience. Imprint it in your brain. Take particular note of those areas that needed to be adjusted. Now, turn your attention back to your breathing. Notice how much freer and deeper it is in this stance.

Be sure to work on your posture for seated speaking as well. Resist the tendency to cave in at the waist. You will feel energized by your enhanced breath, elongated spine, and strengthened voice.

Let the Breath Do the Work

As speakers, we are fooled into thinking we produce our voices by actively manipulating the muscles of the larynx, much as we might activate our legs playing hopscotch. But in fact, phonation, or sound production, is essentially a passive, aerodynamic process. As the column of air from the diaphragm passes through the voice box or larynx, it sets the vocal cords vibrating, generating sound waves. Many speakers exert themselves unnecessarily by trying to use the muscles of the neck and larynx to do the work of the column of air. Such habits result in vocal fatigue, frequent laryngitis, and a harsh-sounding voice. It is important to relax the neck and larynx and keep them entirely passive, which allows the diaphragm to provide the airflow that does all the work.

Exercise: First, check your posture, head position, and breath. Keeping the head aligned with the spine is essential. Avoid hanging your head back with shoulders rolled forward and chin jutting forward (a position many people unconsciously adopt when working at a computer or using a phone). Contrast the feeling of the correct alignment, when the neck is flexed and relaxed, with the jutting or tense position, when the neck becomes tight and tense. Place the fingers of one hand gently on either side of your larynx, where the Adam's apple protrudes, and gently wiggle it back and forth, first in the jutting/tense position, then in the aligned/relaxed position. Notice how much freer it is and how easily it can move in the aligned position.

Now, from this relaxed, aligned position, begin a big yawn with your mouth wide open as you take in the air. Allow the sound of a gentle sigh to float out as you exhale. Prolong this gentle "*ahhhh*" with each exhalation. Test the muscles again by gently moving your larynx with your hand, and try to keep them relaxed even while speaking. Try saying a breathy syllable upon each exhalation: "*Ha. Hay. Ho. Who. He.*" Notice how relaxed and open you can keep your throat and how effortlessly the sound floats out. Try to keep this easy, relaxed feeling as you count to 10.

Producing sounds in this relaxed way both enhances the aesthetic quality of your voice and increases your stamina. The beauty of a highly trained speaker's voice comes from her ability to relax and allow both vocal cords to vibrate harmoniously. Tension disrupts this harmony.

Control the Breath

Suggesting that you control your breath seems to contradict the preceding advice, which was to let your breath do the work. But think what it means to ride a horse. The horse does the work, but you have to keep it from galloping away with you. When the breath is not under control, you are likely to run out of it. If you think of your lungs as bellows that work best by steady and frequent replenishment without ever totally emptying, you may better understand the need to be aware of how much air you have left at any given point in your talk. Many speakers try to produce overly long utterances on one breath. Read the last few paragraphs of this chapter out loud, and notice how many phrases you try to speak without breathing in. Now read the paragraph again with frequent pauses, and remember to take a sip of air during each pause. As you learn to provide better breath support, you will notice an improvement in volume and voice quality.

Avoid fading by running out of air. Make sure you breathe and project through to the very last syllable of each word and paragraph. If this is difficult for you, practice matching the breath to the phrase by counting and interspersing the intervals with a little sip of air, as explained in the exercise below:

Exercise: First count to 10 several times as follows: *1, 2, 3, 4, 5, 6, 7, 8, 9, 10*, sip, *1, 2, 3, 4, 5, 6, 7, 8, 9, 10*, sip, *1, 2, 3, 4, 5, 6, 7, 8, 9, 10*, sip, *1, 2, 3, 4, 5, 6, 7, 8, 9, 10*, sip. You should be able to continue indefinitely, without stress or strain, if you are matching the breath to the phrase. Now count to five as many times as you can: *1, 2, 3, 4, 5*, sip, *1, 2, 3, 4, 5*, sip, *1, 2, 3, 4, 5*, sip. If you become light-headed or feel as if you are about to float away, you may be taking in too much air. Try it again. Now try mixing the intervals, always speaking on one smooth exhalation with little sips of air at the pauses: *1, 2, 3, 4, 5*, sip, *1, 2, 3*, sip, *1, 2, 3, 4, 5, 6, 7*, sip, *1, 2, 3, 4, 5*, sip, *1, 2, 3, 4, 5, 6, 7, 8, 9, 10*, sip, *1, 2*, sip, *1, 2, 3*, and so on.

MANAGE PITCH, VOLUME, AND PACING
TO GET AND KEEP ATTENTION

Even if your voice is pleasant and relaxed, the content of your presentation will be lost on your audience if you cannot hold their attention with your voice. Have you ever heard someone speak in a monotone? Can you imagine having to sit through a 20-minute presentation with such a speaker? Of course, a speaker is never literally monotonic. But to be an effective speaker, you must vary your pitch, volume, and the pace and duration to guarantee that the audience will remain with you throughout your presentation. You may recall from Chapter 4 that the human brain is designed to attend to novel stimuli and ignore ongoing, unchanging background noise, such as the hum of the refrigerator. So if you speak in an *unvarying* tone, at a *constant* volume, at an *unchanging* rate, or in a *predictable* singsong pattern, the listener will find it increasingly difficult to stay tuned in. You must become aware of the ways in which you lapse into less-than-stimulating speech patterns without knowing you are doing it. Then play with these elements as though you were creating a wonderful piece of music, with different movements of allegro and adagio, with moods of tremolo and crescendo. Ideally you express each phrase with a new inflection and tone to convey the nuance you intend.

Use Pauses Generously and Regulate Rate Prudently

Just as the "rests" are important in a piece of music and blank spaces on a page are important to good graphic design, pauses are an important part of your speech pattern and rhythm. Confident, polished speakers use pauses to add emphasis and meaning to their message. (*pause*) Can you see how the pause provides time and space for you to process what you have read? And another thing about pauses (*pause*): They add drama and capture your attention the same way **bold face type** does. Gain comfort with the silence engendered by pauses. Avoid fillers, such as "*um, er, you know.*" As the speaker, you, too, can benefit from the pause by using the moment to recenter your breathing and your thoughts.

Your rate of speech also impacts the listener. If you speak too rapidly, she will feel fatigued and stressed. If you speak too slowly, her attention becomes labored, causing irritation. Try reading this section of the chapter out loud, beginning with the subtitle and going through to the end of this sentence. Time yourself. You should read it in approximately one minute, as it contains approximately 160 words. The average rate of speaking is 145 to 175 wpm (words per minute), with the ideal at about 155 to 160 wpm, depending on the subject matter and occasion.

Find Your Optimal Pitch

Each syllable we speak can be played as a note on a musical instrument. Indeed, a phrase is like the melody of a song. If you hum a few familiar phrases without the words, they would still be recognizable by their tune. Your habitual pitch is the note you most frequently use as you jump up for emphasis and move down to end the phrases, plus it serves as your "neutral" starting point. Many speech coaches mistakenly advise speakers to lower this pitch to achieve a stronger voice. This is hazardous advice. Each person must use the pitch determined by the physical dimensions of her vocal cords. Otherwise she may set up a pattern of abuse and misuse that can result in vocal polyps or nodules, chronic hoarseness, and fatigue. And she will not have relaxed, easy access to a desired range of pitches needed for pleasing variety and expressiveness. There are healthy ways to cultivate a richer, more powerful-sounding voice, which you will discover in the exercises below, especially in the section showing you how to "Turn Up the Bass." Your optimal pitch allows you to create sound without strain or tension.

> **Exercise:** Try gently saying *"mm 'hmm"* out loud, right now, in a relaxed and neutral, rather than expressive, voice. Keep it at about the same pitch as a gentle (very gentle) cough. This is your neutral, optimal pitch. Notice how relaxed your throat feels as this *mm 'hmm* floats out. Now intersperse the gentle *"mm 'hmm"* with counting: *"mm 'hmm 1, mm 'hmm 2, mm 'hmm 3, mm 'hmm 4. . . ."* Keep going all the way to 10. Notice what happened on the numbers. Did your pitch rise or sink? The numbers are typically said at your habitual pitch, the pitch you use in conversation. Was it different from your neutral, optimal *mm 'hmm* pitch?

If you were to create a chart that listed your full vocal range, from the lowest pitch you can comfortably produce to the highest, you would find your optimal pitch at about one-quarter of the way above your lowest note. This means that you can comfortably use three or four notes below your best pitch and between six and eight notes above, providing a dynamic range of ten to thirteen notes for expressive speech. The upper half of your range is available for singing, but we don't generally use those high notes in speech. Try the following method to identify your optimal pitch and see if it matches the one you discovered with the *"mm 'hmm"* method above:

> **Exercise:** Using the syllable *La*, sing down to the lowest note that is comfortable for you. Then begin on that lowest note and sing up the scale by counting, saying the numbers on each note: 1, 2, 3, 4, 5, 6, 7, 8, 9. You will notice that your voice seems to

break through easily on one of the numbers, probably around 4 or 5. This should prove to be your most comfortable note. Try it again. When you are sure where the breakthrough note occurs, continue repeating that clearest, easiest note as though you were chanting, using the syllable *La, la, la. . . .* Try saying entire sentences on this same pitch. *"This is my optimal pitch. Here I am comfortable and clear-voiced."* Continue until you can stop and begin again on the same pitch without having to go through the range of notes.

Your optimal pitch is your starting point or home base. It is like a pitch pipe helping you to find your key. From there you will modulate when it is appropriate for emphasis or inference, but you will always return to your starting point. You may find that it seems higher (or lower) than the pitch you are accustomed to using for speech. But by practicing and modifying your pitch even slightly toward the optimum, you help eliminate vocal burnout or problems with a voice that is unpleasant or hard to hear. Try beginning these sentences at your optimal pitch by starting with a gentle *"mm 'hmm"*:

> *"mm 'hmm It's a beautiful day."*
> *"mm 'hmm She's a wonderful speaker."*
> *"mm 'hmm That's an interesting idea."*

Does your voice sound and feel different than when you use your habitual pitch? This slight adjustment in pitch makes a dramatic difference for some speakers.

Use this *"mm 'hmm"* technique as a guide when you begin speaking. You may find that sometimes, especially when you are nervous or excited, tension builds up in the throat and you end up speaking at an extreme of your pitch range. Your voice comes out screechy or squeaky and adds to your nervousness. If you remember to stop, center, breathe, and imagine yourself saying "*mm 'hmm*," you will get off to a much better start by speaking at your optimal pitch.

VARY YOUR PITCH

Now that you have found your optimal pitch, you are ready to experiment with a variety of pitches within your normal range, which will add interest to your speech. Unemotional, factual speech that is appropriate for everyday occasions includes a range of ten notes—three below, one at, and six above the optimum, or modal pitch. When the speaking situation is more emotional or personal, it becomes appropriate to extend the range to thirteen notes by going higher by two more notes and lower by one. If you reduce the range to just seven notes by cutting off the upper tones, you might sound apathetic. If you reduce it by cutting off the lower tones, you risk sounding indecisive and lacking in confidence. If you restrict the range to four or five notes, you give the impression of speaking in a monotone.

Imagine all the possible ways to say "Please sit down." First, picture the speaker as relaxed, calm, and speaking politely to an honored guest:

"Please sit down."

Now, imagine her commanding an errant student with considerable exasperation and anger after several requests:

"Puleeease sit dowwwwwnnnnnn!"

What are the differences? Pitch, plus volume, rate, and tone quality are used with a much greater range in the latter, angry example. The duration of each syllable and pause between is longer, everything is louder, the first word is higher in pitch, and the final word is lower in pitch. The tone of voice is gentle and relaxed in the first case, whereas it is brittle and harsh in the latter. How you vary your voice has a great deal to do with how your meaning is received.

CONVEY AUTHORITY AND CONFIDENCE USING APPROPRIATE PITCH

As we discussed earlier, the absence of the higher (also louder and longer) notes conveys apathy. As you listen to various speakers in the coming weeks, notice that they convey emotion, especially positive enthusiasm, by jumping up in pitch and making some syllables louder and longer. Note also that they convey certainty and credibility by controlling the pitch and ending statements with a downward inflection. The following exercise allows you to use your own voice to hear how important appropriate pitch is:

> **Exercise:** Read aloud the sentence below, following the pitch levels indicated. Compare the impression each leaves:

Rising inflection: indecisive

```
          ver           tant
This        y    por
     is       im
```

Falling inflection: definite

```
          ver
This        y    por
     is       im
                      tant
```

Did you notice how the absence of the lower tones imparts indecisiveness and a lack of authority? Leaving the last syllable at a neutral or rising pitch leaves the thought hanging uncertainly, as though suspended in midair. When a thought is complete and an idea is firmly held, you must drop the pitch at the end of the sentence. The rising inflection is appropriate for yes/no questions, such as "Does this make sense?" The listener will feel compelled to create closure by providing the downward inflection with their firm "yes" or "no." But if the rising pattern is used in a statement, you reduce the impact of the idea.

In addition to ending your sentences with a clear fall in pitch, it is vital to project your voice through the very last syllable. Don't swallow your words or fade out at the end of sentences as so many speakers do. Remember to use good breath support and keep the air flowing *out* and down, like a wave. Don't allow the last word to fall *back* and down.

An important time to remember these guidelines is whenever you introduce yourself. Have you ever noticed how difficult it is to catch somebody's name? When you have never met a person before, her name is an abstraction because there are no associations to help you remember it. Yet most of us tend to hurry through our names and fade away in a flat or rising tone, as if apologizing or questioning who we are.

                        Partnow
      I'm Susan
  Hi

Contrast that weak introduction with this one, saying it slowly, firmly, strongly:

      I'm   *Part*
  Hi   *Su*
          san
              now

Try this exercise with your name. If your name is unusual, be sure to pause slightly after your first name to help the listener distinguish your first name from your last name.

Crank Up the Volume to Energize Your Audience

When you speak before a group, the listeners are inclined to match their energy level with the energy conveyed by your voice. Volume is one measure of energy, so it is almost always advisable to crank up the volume beyond your usual estimation of what is appropriate. I think of my voice as the battery supplying all the "juice" in the room. Of course, you must adjust the level according to the number of people listening. If a small group of people is sitting close to you, you can speak more softly than if a large group fills a large room. But remember, you want to make it *easy* for the listeners to hear you, not just possible. Louder is better.

Be sure to vary the loudness with which you speak. Really punch out the key words and phrases. To see how good you are at it, try speaking into a tape recorder that has a volume meter. See if your voice makes the dial move dynamically, with some phrases quieter, some louder. Remember, however, to let your breath do the work in regulating volume. Forcing volume from the muscles around your vocal chords produces only a screech. Bringing volume up from your diaphragm produces a pleasing sense of authority in your voice.

Project Your Voice Where You Want It

Where do you direct your voice when you are speaking? Obviously, in one-on-one conversations, you stand or sit facing your partner and speak loudly enough for her to hear you easily. When you are speaking before a group, you have to project your voice in a way that makes it easy for every person in the room to hear you. Projection becomes a matter not just of volume but also of tone and focus. Think of filling the room with your voice, sending every sound you make to the back of the room, to reach the ears of the farthest listener. Many speakers have a tendency to "speak into their collar," as a Spanish saying goes, holding the voice close to the body.

> **Exercise:** Experiment with this notion of focusing your voice. First try saying a sentence close to your body. Don't whisper, but, in a normal tone, speak "into your collar," saying, *"I'm holding my voice right here."* Now aim your voice toward someone across the room and, without shouting or *trying* to speak louder, say, *"And now I'm sending my voice to you."* Can you feel and hear the difference? Try the two phrases again. First the wrong way, then the desired way. Do you see how focusing your voice properly helps it to fill the room? Develop an awareness of where your voice is focused at all times, and then, whenever you are speaking to a group, aim your voice out, towards the listener who is farthest away.

While doing the above experiment with focus and tone, you may have noticed that your mouth and throat opened more, allowing the air to flow more freely. Increased airflow allows the voice to be heard more easily, even at lower volumes. These are good voice habits. Yet, when asked to speak loudly, you may find yourself using different voice habits. Let's try another experiment.

> **Exercise:** First, speak in your usual voice, but notice the pattern of your breath and the sensations in the muscles of your throat, neck, and diaphragm. Say, *"How does this feel?"* Remember these sensations. Next, try speaking in a very loud voice, and notice what you do to increase the volume by paying attention to how your breath, throat, mouth, and jaw *feel*. Imagine that you are speaking so loudly that the people in the next room will hear you. Say, *"Hello out there!"* How did you make your voice louder? Did you push harder in your neck and tighten your throat? Although this works, it is a form of vocal abuse that can damage your vocal cords. Ideally, you will have noticed that you

pushed harder from the diaphragm, sending out more air more quickly while you actually relaxed and opened your throat and mouth. Indeed, using your mouth like a megaphone to amplify the sound is a healthy way to project your voice.

TURN UP THE BASS

Most people do not like the way they sound on a tape recording. Indeed, many do not even recognize their voice when they hear it for the first time. Rest assured, the recording *does* sound different from the way you hear yourself because when you speak, you hear yourself through bone conduction *and* through air waves. When you hear yourself on a recording, you can hear yourself only through the air waves. The recorded signal seems tinnier and higher in pitch. Because bones are excellent conductors of bass tones, a recording misses a rich component that you are accustomed to hearing in your own voice. But brace yourself. That tinniness is the way others hear you. Alas, they can't hear the bones vibrating in your head. If you want others to hear you the way you hear yourself, you have to turn up the bass in your voice.

The sound waves generated at the level of the vocal cords are actually quite feeble. As they pass through your throat and mouth, they are amplified. The way you position your jaw, tongue, and lips along with the contour of your throat profoundly affect the output of sound. Sound waves have a physical reality to them, with variation in depth and length according to frequency. Low, bass tones are big and long, and they require a lot of space. Treble tones are small and short. Imagine a row of jars before you, graduated in size from very small to very large. Which one produces a low, bass tone when you tap it? The large jar can accommodate the larger sound waves of the lower frequencies. The sounds we produce are equally affected by the volume of space we create in our vocal tract. A third element that impacts the mix of bass and treble in your voice is the texture of the walls of the resonating chamber. You know that woodwinds are soft and permeable and produce a mellow tone, whereas brass instruments are hard and reflective. The sound waves literally bounce off the hard walls, thus creating an excess of the smaller high-frequency treble tones. The walls of your throat impact the tone in the same way. You will sound brassy if your throat is tense, mellow if you are relaxed.

Let's experiment and see what we can do to maximize that mellow "FM" sound and minimize a thin, tinny, brassy sound:

> **Exercise:** Prolong a gentle "*ahhhh*" sound, well supported by breath. Keep the sound going while you slowly open and close your mouth. Notice how the tone quality changes. Which sounds deeper and fuller? The open position, right? Now you have the first key to a resonant voice: Get your mouth and throat open! Next contrast the tone quality produced when you pucker your lips and say "*ooo*" (rhymes with two) with the sound of "*eee*" (rhymes with tea) with your lips pulled back, almost in a grin. Can you hear it? When you add the length of the lips to the vocal tract, the sound is much richer, full of bass tones. The second key to a resonant voice: Use your lips to round the sounds. Try saying the following phrases while striving for a different feeling in your throat. First say, "*I am feeling stressed and edgy,*" while tensing the back of your throat. Now say, "*My throat is opened and relaxed,*" with the throat velvety and relaxed. Did you notice the change in tone quality? This sense of relaxed softness is the third key to a resonant voice.

Integrate the following habits into your speech patterns. Try reading a poem aloud while you practice each one. Go back to the earlier exercise on saying your name and add these elements to the downward inflection you were practicing:

- Open the mouth and throat *to expand volume.*
- Activate the lips and round the vowels *to add length.*
- Relax the throat *to soften and mellow the voice.*

When films or plays caricature a woman as a "dumb blonde," they often portray her with a thin voice. Carol Channing has played such a character in the movies *The First Traveling Saleslady* and *Thoroughly Modern Millie.* She sounded young, immature, and not very credible. You might remember her trademark wide, toothy smile? With that grin she sacrificed length and volume to the vocal tract and thus turned up the treble in her voice. So, ladies, smile with your eyes but use those lips to round your vowels.

Many people hold tension in their jaws, making it difficult to speak with an open throat. Do you tend to grit your teeth or grind them at night? Notice how they are right now while you are reading. Are they slightly apart, or are you clenching them? The only time your teeth need to touch each other is when you are chewing. Try to increase the space between the back molars to help get your throat as open as possible, like an inverted megaphone with the widest point at the back of your mouth and the narrow point at the lips. Many of my students think of this as orienting their speech in a vertical north-south plane, rather than the typical American horizontal east-west twang. I think of it as my "French face" because it's the facial posture I use to speak with a French accent. Some voice coaches have students practice with a slice of cork between the back teeth to encourage this posture. Try this gentle stretch:

> **Exercise:** First, become aware of the tension in your jaw joint, the hinge where the lower jaw, or mandible, attaches to the skull. Say *"Oh, Oh, Oh,"* several times while you turn your attention to this area. Then allow your jaw to drop open in a relaxed way, as if to say *"AHH."* Now keep the jaw open while you

move lips only to form the *"Oh."* Does the jaw joint feel freer to move? Just this slight shift, a kind of release to allow the jaw to slide forward, can help relax the jaw and allow you to increase the internal volume, which in turn enhances the bass, mellow quality of your voice.

INCREASE YOUR STAMINA

Are you suffering from vocal burnout? How many of the following symptoms do you experience?

- Tired or strained voice.
- Frequent throat clearing or coughing.
- Rawness or burning in throat.
- Sensation of lump or tickling in throat.
- Pain or discomfort in throat or neck area.
- Dry or scratchy throat and mouth.
- Frequent sore throats.
- Hoarseness or huskiness.
- Voice breaks or skips.
- Weakening or loss of voice.
- Change in voice quality vs. a year or two ago.
- Reduced pitch range.
- Neck muscles bulging or tense.
- Avoidance of speaking situations.

You may want to seek the services of a certified speech therapist to work on changing your voice habits if you experience many of these symptoms chronically. In fact, if you suffer hoarseness that persists for more than two weeks without an infection, you should consult an ear, nose, and throat specialist. If medical examination reveals any tissue change in your vocal cords, medical insurance and/or workers' compensation may cover voice therapy. If good speech is essential for current employment, voice training may be a tax deductible business expense. You can find speech therapists listed in the yellow pages or through larger hospitals. Make sure they are certified by the American Speech-Language-Hearing Association (CCC–Certificate of Clinical Competence).

In addition to practicing breath support and relaxation, and using proper head alignment and optimum pitch as described above, there are many things you can do to enhance the durability of your voice on your own. Try observing these guidelines:

• **Keep the vocal tract moist.** Maintain humidity in your environment and drink lots of water.

• **Eliminate misuses.** Frequent throat clearing, screaming, harsh laughter, grunts, or guttural sounds aggravate the vocal cords.

• **Control abuses.** Alcohol and cigarettes are irritants to the vocal tract.

• **Manage the sound environment.** Eliminate competing noises, turn down the radio, and refrain from lengthy conversations in noisy environments, such as cars or planes.

• **Practice moderation.** Avoid speaking at unusually high or low pitches or volumes. Use amplification when appropriate; allow the voice to rest before and after speaking on demanding days.

Here's another voice tip: As for any other muscles in the body, you can prevent vocal strain and promote better performance by warming up. Have you noticed how froglike you sound first thing in the morning? Try this exercise as a warm-up routine:

Exercise: A good warm-up routine begins with a posture and breathing check, and then gentle humming that moves your voice up and down the scale, as for arpeggios. Vary the vowel. Start going up the scale as for do, me, sol, ti: "me, me, me, me"; now head down the scale as for sol, me, do: "me, me, me"; then "ma, ma, ma, ma, ma, ma, ma," and so forth, continuing with "moe" and "moo." Try some phrases that get your lips lively and your mouth open, "How now brown cow" and "The rain in Spain stays mainly on the plain." Next try some tongue twisters to awake your tongue to crisp sounds: "Tickle Tune Typhoon sings the best songs for tots."

These suggested adjustments to your voice are challenging. Don't expect to use them all of the time. In fact, wait until you have mastered a new pattern in practice sessions before trying them out in the real world. Aim for frequent but short practice sessions. Two or three minutes of practice implemented numerous times throughout the day are much more effective than one session of twenty to thirty minutes. When you practice, keep your standards high by urging yourself to exaggerate. Each time you repeat a phrase in practice, define the goal narrowly, and then judge each of your attempts to determine whether you are meeting the goal. Set small, specific goals for each practice sentence so that you plan for success, not failure. For example, if you are trying to increase resonance, lower your pitch at the end of phrases, and improve projection, focus on just one of these components at a time. Close attention and awareness of how it feels to produce the new pattern will maximize the effectiveness of your practice sessions.

Reading out loud is an excellent way to practice new patterns. Poetry and plays are especially suited for oral practice, but you can use whatever material you are currently reading. Write up lists of key phrases that you use in a typical day. Read a sentence several times, each time zeroing in on a different goal. For example, the first time just think about getting your mouth open. Next, work on posture and breath support through to the very last syllable. Then pay attention to round-ing the vowels and really using your lips. Now read it again, putting all three patterns together. Keep a card with practice phrases in your briefcase or purse, or clip one to the visor of your car. Whenever you are waiting in line, stopped at a red light, or walking alone, take the opportunity to practice enhancing your voice patterns. Once a week, get out your tape recorder and practice until you can hear a noticeable improvement.

When you are ready to bring the patterns into the "real world," choose a particular time during your day when you can give your voice your full attention in a speaking situation. A phone call that you initiate is a good place to practice. If you are unsure, think about the phrases you are likely to use and practice modulating your voice ahead of time. Feel successful just for trying and being focused on your goal for those few minutes. All this hard work will pay off. Before you know it, you will begin to notice improvement. Then, week by week, you will get better and better. Congratulations! You are learning to put your best voice forward.

Part III

Finishing Touches and Accessories

STAND AND DELIVER

Meet the challenge of formal presentations by incorporating these basics.

The manner of your speaking is full as
important as the matter, as more people
have ears to be tickled than
understanding to judge.
—LORD CHESTERFIELD,
SEVENTEENTH-CENTURY STATESMAN

Now that you have polished the content of your speech and improved the quality of your voice, you are ready to turn your attention to the most vital visual aid that is available to every
speaker: your body and your face. Whether intentionally or
unconsciously, your body and face are broadcasting strong
messages on every channel, which the audience receives
whenever you speak. In order to convince listeners of your message, you must reinforce your ideas and let the passion show in
your eyes, your facial expression, and your gestures. In other
words, *you* are your own best visual aid.

Consider these facts: UCLA researcher Albert Mehrabian
has determined that the verbal component, or scripted words,
of any speaker's presentation accounts for only 7 percent of the
impact the presentation makes on the audience. The vocal
component of tone and inflection accounts for 38 percent of
the impact, and what the audience members *see* comprises a
whopping 55 percent of how they respond to the presentation.
Michael Argyle, a British researcher, believes that nonverbal
cues have four to six times the effect of verbal cues in affecting
listeners' attitudes. These numbers offer a crucial lesson for
you as a speaker: Pay careful attention to your delivery, and
learn to present yourself skillfully. If there is any discrepancy
between the nonverbal and verbal cues, the listener will heed

the nonverbal signals. They generate more credibility than the words. *You* are the message. *How* you speak is louder than what you say.

USE YOUR NATURAL TALENTS

How can you master the art of an effective delivery? The most important thing is to relax and let your best self shine through, knowing that you are naturally endowed with the capability to enhance your words with your face and gestures. If you think about it, you will realize that you learned the vocabulary of nonverbal communication at your family's kitchen table. You do not have to become someone else, and you certainly don't have to memorize artificial gestures in order to be a successful speaker. You only need to approach every speaking situation as though you were at that kitchen table enjoying a rousing debate or storytelling session with your family and friends.

For many women, the ability to approach speaking this way is more easily said than done. The natural charisma most women are blessed with goes out the window in speaking situations because of self-consciousness. But you already have most of the tools you need to foil self-consciousness without adopting an artificial style. You know how to manage your nervousness by remembering to *stop, center, breathe,* and *relax.* You know how to develop the content of your presentation so that you feel confident and prepared. And you have practiced projecting the splendid voice you began cultivating in the last chapter. Keep your affirmations and positive visualizations in mind. Now, read on to polish the skills you need to captivate your listeners by using eye contact, facial expressions, natural hand gestures, body postures, and movement.

Speak from Your Heart to Their Eyes

While your voice projects your words, it is your eyes that hold your audience. Without eye contact you will, at best, undermine your message. At worst, you'll lose your audience altogether. Indeed, if you do not make direct eye contact, listeners might suspect that you are unsure of yourself, disinterested, or even dishonest. But when you do make eye contact, you need also to be aware of the message your eyes are conveying. Charlotte Brontë once observed that "The soul . . . has an interpreter—often an unconscious, but still a truthful interpreter— in the eye."

Without your necessarily being aware of it, your eyes work to communicate powerful signals about your state of mind, your emotion and intention, your competence and ability. Blinking rapidly or holding a steady gaze, rolling your eyes, cutting them to the right and left, widening or narrowing them, letting them shine with interest or "glaze over"—all reveal how you feel about the subject at hand or the people with whom you are speaking. You may sabotage your message if your gaze doesn't fit the pattern that the audience recognizes as normal. So it is well to be aware, not just of making eye contact, but of what your eyes are "doing."

Making eye contact while standing before a group of people is not much different from making contact in a one-on-one speaking situation. When sitting and talking with a friend, if you are looking out the window, up at the ceiling, or down at your feet, she will feel excluded and irrelevant. Looking at her, on the other hand, is like calling her by name. It keeps her attention and makes her feel interested. The same holds true for a group of people. The only difference is that you have to vary the direction of your gaze, so that as many people as possible are touched by your desire to make them feel included. Fortunately, *where* you turn your gaze while speaking is completely under your control.

Notice how you direct your gaze the next time you share a meal with a group of friends. Observe how eye contact draws attention to you by engaging the receiver of your message. Notice how you respond to another speaker when she makes frequent eye contact with you. How do you feel if the speaker does not make that contact? At the next meeting you attend, pay attention to whether the speaker looks only at one or two important people in the room, or if she makes all the participants feel that what she says is relevant to them.

In large groups, you don't need to lock eyes with every person, but you want every person to feel as if she has been noticed. In fact, you want to establish eye contact *before* you even begin speaking. While you are being introduced, or while you are waiting for the meeting to come to order, mentally divide the audience into quadrants, and scan each section by making direct contact with different people within it. As your talk progresses, this technique will prevent your giving attention only to the high-priced orchestra seats held by the VIPs in the group or tending to a favored part of the room. Be inclusive. Don't let anyone feel left out. If the audience is quite large, establish more sections.

When you follow this advice to scan the room in sections, however, avoid falling into a repetitive scanning pattern. You may have seen speakers who seem robotlike as they sweep their eyes over the audience. They broadcast insincerity and detachment, and ultimately distract people from their message. You want to draw your listeners *to* you, not to *oversee* them. Keep your pattern smooth, natural, and unpredictable. Allow your gaze to rest for several seconds before moving to another person. You can often detect a slight gesture of response as an individual feels noticed. Imagine that you are gathering new friends as you move from one individual to the next. This warm approach will bring a smile to your lips and a softness to your eyes. Remember, moreover, that your voice tends to follow your eyes, so that improving your eye contact with the audience will often improve voice projection.

> **Exercise:** Go to the largest room in your home or office. Stand where you would deliver an announcement. Pick out six or seven spots in the room where you imagine your listeners would be sitting. You might want to position lamps, chairs, or candlesticks as "audience members." Utilize all four corners of the room, all the walls, and the center front, middle, and back. Now begin talking to your audience. Pick out an imaginary person. Imagine seeing her. Imagine her responsive eyes connecting with yours. Now move to the next listener, talking all the while. Use a varied pattern so that you are not rotating your head back and forth. (This is not a tennis match!) Take your time. Allow yourself to feel relaxed and dynamically connected to each of these attentive "listeners." Be like a gracious hostess, offering each person you look at a tasty morsel of your remarks, as if you were serving a tray of hors d'oeuvres at a party. Keep speaking until you've had a chance to make contact with all seven "listeners" several times each.

Play with eye contact whenever you are in a sizable room. Mentally, deliver a meaningful message you would like to share with people in different sections of the room. If you're at a concert, walk up to the front of the concert hall during intermission, turn around and face "your audience." Give yourself two minutes to imagine you are about to address the crowd. How will you divide the room?

Let the Enthusiasm Show in Your Face

Be aware that as you speak, your listener is continuously reading your face. Eyes, brows, forehead, mouth—even your nose—play a part. You want your sincerity and enthusiasm to show. If you find when practicing a presentation that your face remains passive, consider the possibility that your are not paying close enough attention to your words. You need to connect your heart, as well as your head, to your message. But you don't need to *try* to be expressive. As long as you are genuinely concerned about getting your message across, and you remain aware of what you are saying, the appropriate facial expression will appear.

There is one facial expression you should plan to work on: your *smile!* A warm smile creates a strong signal to your audience that you are friendly, reliable, glad to be there, and pleasant to be around. And it makes *you* feel good, too, providing just the boost of confidence and energy you need to begin with positive momentum. The simple act of smiling in a way that lights up your eyes stimulates the release of endorphins, those body chemicals so essential to feeling good. Smiling also helps loosen up your facial muscles. So, unless you are dealing with a gloomy issue, smile often. Let your face beam with energy, pleasure, and warmth. But do remember to use your lips to round your sounds.

Certain facial expressions can detract from your presentation, especially those that announce your mistakes! In my classes I often observe speakers who wince and grimace when they forget a thought or mispronounce a word. Watch out for eye rolling and shoulder shrugging, too. Why draw the audience's attention to your little flaws? Without all the drama, they probably will never be noticed! Let your expression broadcast a clear message: "I am glad to be here. I am poised and powerful." Never let a frown or sigh escape that transmits "Let's get this over with," or "I hate doing this."

Eye contact creates a reciprocal relationship. When you see a listener looking eagerly at you, you automatically reflect that eagerness, and you feel inspired to give her more of what she is enjoying. However, be aware that most speakers, no matter how thrilling their subject, experience audiences who sit passively throughout a talk, giving the impression that they are not taking anything in. Bland expressions may reflect cultural differences or differences in personality and may not mean people are unexcited by your message. You must be on guard against the contagion of reflecting their blankness on your own face. Look at passive audience members as a challenge and a call for more energy. If your own animation elicits responses, you can be proud of your ability to overcome a listener's neutral expression.

I recall a particularly challenging group of predominantly male engineers. Their lack of overt responsiveness felt like a black hole, absorbing all my energy. I felt my anxiety rise until I gave the group a few minutes to talk in small groups and then elicited their remarks. Once I could evoke a response and confirm their interest, I was able to charge ahead, uncontaminated by their lack of animation.

Speak with Your Whole Body

We learned how important it is to vary your voice so that you won't be tuned out as background noise. It is equally important for you to vary your physical stance. The way you use the space around you broadcasts a strong message.

What does your posture say? If you slouch, it says you are dull and unconcerned. If you are stiff, it expresses tension, unfriendliness, and inflexibility. If you pace or sway, it announces nervousness and self absorption. If you lean, it declares dependence. What you want is a stance that reflects relaxed, alert competence and allows flowing, natural movement. It's the same posture that fosters good breath support.

Begin with an upright posture: back straight, feet slightly apart, knees slightly bent, and hands relaxed at your sides. Feel as though you are suspended from a plumb line attached to the crown of your head. Keep your weight on both feet so that you are solidly grounded. (I avoid high heels because they make me feel off balance and less powerful.) Think of this as your neutral or default position, and return to it often. If you are seated at a meeting or an informal gathering, posture is still important. Remain erect and alert as you speak. Imagine yourself lifted from the waist, rather than sunken in. This posture helps your breathing, too. You may want to lean slightly forward, toward your listeners, and keep your hands above table level, resting lightly on the chair arms or table top, if you like. If there is no cloth on the table, or no table at all, watch those knees! The speaker's platform is not a good place for short skirts.

Make *use* of the space around you. You are not a statue. Your talk is *live*, so move! If you move confidently around the room, you generate positive energy, even dynamic tension, as the listeners anticipate your physical approach. You also continually establish your role as an active leader. Make sure you move purposefully, linking your movements to your meaning, if possible. For example, it is natural to introduce a new idea by taking a few steps to a new spot. There may be brief times when you remain stationary, even leaning lightly on a table behind you while you settle in for some of the general discussion. But return to your upright, default position to summarize. Be sure to begin and end your talk—as well as each major section—in this more powerful and well-balanced position. Watch for such distracting habits as pacing, swaying, shifting, rocking, toe tapping, and heel grinding (very tempting in those stiletto heels).

Have you ever found yourself backing up from someone who was standing too close as she spoke to you? You might say she invaded your personal boundaries. In our North American culture, we reserve the bubble of space within about 4 feet of our bodies as accessible only for intimate others. This space extends from 4 to about 12 feet for everyday interactions with colleagues and friends. We like to keep strangers beyond 12 feet. As speakers, we must respect the spatial boundaries that people unconsciously place around them. Maintain a distance of 6 to 7 feet from the front row of your audience—less if they know you well. If you invade the personal space more intimately, you will make the people uncomfortable and they will cease attending to your message. On the other hand, if you stay too far away from your audience, beyond 12 feet, you are casting them into the public space outside the zone of your influence. This may make you appear unfriendly, uncomfortable, uncertain—and unconnected.

Variety is indispensable to a successful delivery style. Just as you've learned to do with your vocal habits, orchestrate a repertory of movements, and tie them to the ideas you are expressing. Pay attention to the rhythm and pacing, the way a conductor coordinates musicians playing a complex piece of music. Don't forget to make use of dramatic pauses, allowing your whole body to stop moving in order to heighten the effect. And keep smiling.

Lend a Hand

Some of us were told as youngsters that it was rude to talk with our hands. Times have changed! With the advent of television, communication has become increasingly visual. Have you seen film clips of the first televised presidential debate, between Kennedy and Nixon back in 1960? They stayed behind the podium the whole time and you almost never saw their hands. Compare that with the 1996 debate where Clinton worked the stage like a seasoned talk-show host.

There is no escaping your hands. They are part of you and must be part of your presentation. If you keep them still, you will miss an opportunity to enhance your talk with memorable visual stimulation. But when you use your hands, the listener's eye is drawn from your face. It is essential, then, to make your gestures enhance your message.

Gesture freely with your whole arm, your head, even your torso at times. Use your hands to emphasize words, illustrate your meaning, and provide symbols. (But be careful—there are cultural differences. For example, the American hand symbol for OK is considered vulgar in some countries!) With a simple gesture you can help display structure, show balance, provide emphasis, and illustrate size, shape, direction, or movement. If you are telling a story about a big man, let your hands and head rise up as you visualize him there. If your anecdote relates righteous anger, put that hand on your hip, let your eyes narrow, your brow frown, your head shake. The more tangibly you evoke the physical presence of some aspect of your topic using gestures and movements, the more your audience will be drawn into your meaning. But avoid limited and repetitive gestures. They can become as distracting and deadening as a monotonous voice.

As with facial expressions, you'll do best to let the gestures happen naturally the way they do when you talk with friends. Don't stage them, because if you do, they'll look and feel contrived and phony. Just keep your arms and hands at the ready, loose and relaxed at your sides. Don't plan specific gestures, but be continually aware of the *need* to gesture. Raise your hands along with your voice. When your gestures occur above the waist, at about chest level, with hands higher than elbows, they appear confident and descriptive, rather than timid or furtive. If you pin your arms tightly to your body, you are limited to insignificant little movements, with hands flapping at your thighs. So relax. Let your gestures be bold. Make them move from the shoulder, not just the elbow, to convey energy.

If you start to feel tense or stiff, take it as an early warning sign and a reminder to *stop, center, breathe,* and *relax.* Avoid stuffing your hands in your pockets or holding them together, causing inertia; it will be hard to make them available again. If you clasp them in front of you "fig-leaf" style, your posture expresses a lack of confidence. If you give in to a tendency to wring your hands, you will offer a rather pathetic picture. If you clasp them behind you, all that's left to gesture with are your shoulders, and you will look like a chicken flapping its wings.

Many of us need literally to stay in touch with ourselves to help us feel grounded. Hence, we cross our arms, clasp our hands, or touch our nose. These unconscious gestures undermine power and credibility. So beware of fidgeting. The act of speaking makes the pulse race and sets off a surge of energy under the most ordinary of circumstances. If you are standing before an audience, the excess flow of energy can be tremendous. Channel this energy out to the audience in purposeful ways—in your confident stride toward them, in your strong voice, your bold gestures, your writing on the board or flip-chart. Don't allow this energy to leak out into twitching or hitching, wiggling or jiggling, squirming or worming. Beware of nearby objects. They will call to you: pens yearning to be clicked, keys to be jingled, tables tapped, hair swirled, rings twirled, ears tugged. These activities may pacify and soothe you, but they'll drive your audience crazy and take them far from your purpose.

If you are uncomfortable with gestures—if your natural style makes little use of them—find some fun ways to explore the realm of body language playfully. Play charades with your family or make up a mime routine for your grandchild. Learn some sign language. Try acting classes or dance lessons. Once you break through your inhibitions, you will develop your own style and vocabulary of gesture.

Practice, Practice, Practice

Most of us have access to a video camera. Ask a family member or friend to videotape you so that you can see how you are doing with eye contact, facial expressions, and gestures. Or at least practice with a mirror and a tape recorder. Everyone else sees you in action; why not take a look, yourself? If you have an upcoming event, invite a few friends and even your dog to join the practice session to help simulate the excitement of having an audience. Setting up the room to resemble the expected situation, and then videotaping, will give you not only a sense of how you move but also a chance to rehearse using any planned props or visual aids.

When you view a videotape of your practice sessions, acknowledge all your strengths and identify habits you want to change. It is useful to get someone else's perspective, so ask your friendly audience for feedback. The emphasis here is on *strengths* and *suggestions.* By identifying all the aspects of your delivery that are good, you can build on them. By identifying specific ways to improve your delivery (without harshly criticizing yourself) you can practice in the newly suggested way. It is counterproductive to focus on what you do "wrong."

If your experience mirrors that of the participants in my workshops, you will be pleasantly surprised to find that you appear less nervous than you feel. Perhaps you'll be surprised to find how gravely serious you look. Next time you'll remember to smile. You may catch yourself making some distracting motions, such as twirling your hair or tugging your ear. Next time you'll remember to gesture purposefully. Make sure you notice how credibly you projected yourself. Appreciate your strong posture and composed expression. Discover how that uncomfortable moment when you forgot a word or stumbled over a name was scarcely perceptible. With this newly discovered awareness—together with patience and persistence—you will continue to improve and polish your speaking style. Use what you learn from the video practice to create a vivid picture of yourself delivering your message even more dynamically and persuasively next time.

MIND YOUR MANNERS

As soon as you are "in range" of any audience members on the site of a presentation, you are "on." If they know who you are, they may be sizing you up even before you are introduced. I realized this principle one day when I arrived at the Seattle Federal Building at the crack of dawn, ready to give a training session. I loved training there because the room was always set up just right and it afforded a great view, amenities that helped compensate for the modest fees paid by the Feds. I was devastated when told that this particular session had been moved to the windowless basement that was stocked with an odd assortment of old tables and chairs. I loaded up my materials and headed for the elevator, grinding my teeth and muttering all the while. My displeasure was quite apparent—and audible. I was so preoccupied with my sulking that I hardly noticed there were others in the elevator. When I reached the training room door and realized that my fellow passengers were my trainees, I was humiliated. I felt that my credibility as a trainer in "Strategies for Success" was deservedly eroded.

I did recover, and the day ended well. But I felt as though I were swimming upstream the whole day. From then on I never forgot: *You're on before you're up!* So resist closing your eyes in a meditative trance or picking your teeth while you're on the sidelines waiting for an introduction. And continue to pay attention to your posture and demeanor as you approach the front of the room.

Further, remember that *you're on even when you're off*. You may have concluded your talk and completed all of your comments, but the audience is still looking at you. Don't roll your eyes, shrug your shoulders, or sigh. Whether delivered verbally or nonverbally, the impression that you are glad the talk is over does not promote your message or enhance your impact. Walk back to your seat with poise. Remain attentive. Be a model, responsive listener.

Dress for the Part

How would you dress for a date with a new admirer? You would carefully consider the occasion, your shared interests, the admirer's expectations. You would make the most of choosing clothing, hairstyle, makeup, and jewelry. To show your interest you would probably dress up. These decisions all form a part of *appearance* communication. When managed wisely in speaking situations, your appearance can add to your power and credibility, gain respect for you and your cause, and create a positive first impression. Of first importance, of course, is careful grooming.

If your presentation is with a group of people you know and interact with on a daily basis, dress as they typically see you. Any radical change could be distracting. If the situation is informal, dress accordingly. Choose clothes that reflect your self-esteem and self-image, your attitude toward your presentation, and your respect for and relationship with the audience. If you want to dress up a little to show your high regard for the listeners, they will appreciate it. But don't overdress for an informal occasion. It would be inappropriate to show up at a bridge club's annual retreat in a business suit if everyone there will be in jeans—unless they have invited you as an outside expert. Then you might choose a nice pair of slacks—informal, but a cut above jeans.

In almost every situation, a conservative approach is usually best. Avoid extreme designs or styles, including sleeveless, strapless, or backless, and keep dresses at knee length unless you want the audience's attention to be on your legs instead of your message. Choose colors and patterns that complement but don't overwhelm you. For a formal presentation, you may want to check out the color behind the podium so that you won't fade into the wallpaper. Keep jewelry to a minimum as it can be distracting, especially large earrings. Consider the impact of any extra lighting that might reflect off your sparkling jewelry, or the distracting sound or swing of any jangling pieces, especially if you will be using a microphone.

Pay attention to your hair style. Does it fall into your face or cover it from the side? I remember attending what should have been a fascinating lecture on the sociology of today's family, but all I could think about was how desperately the speaker needed a haircut as she repeatedly brushed her hair out of her eyes. Consider pinning your hair back to highlight your face. Subtle eye makeup can help the audience make eye contact with you, and lipstick adds a polished look. But avoid unconventional colors for speaking occasions. Manicured nails add a nice touch, but extreme lengths or wild colors draw attention to your hands and detract from your message.

Be sure you are comfortable and at ease with what you wear so that *you* won't be distracted. Give the chosen garment or accessories a "test drive" before wearing them for a speaking date. I was once coldly reminded of what can happen if I don't take my own advice when I wore a new pants suit to a presentation. It was very flattering and slenderizing and looked spectacular in the store mirror. I felt great as I approached the fifty managers assembled for my workshop on "WIN-WIN Communication." However, when I warmed up to my talk and began using the bold gestures I advocate, I felt a distinct breeze that communicated "LOSE-LOSE." I looked down to see my bare midriff peeking out. Next time I'll be sure to wear a teddy underneath.

I blush at the memory of another clothing nightmare. Early on in my speaking days, I was invited to a luncheon in Seattle's swankiest high-rise club. I was to give a presentation titled *Developing Your Professional Sound*, which was meant to complement a fashion show called *Developing Your Professional Look*. The dress store owners who had planned the event had the brilliant idea of letting me model one of the store's gorgeous outfits while I gave my talk.

I drove in that morning wearing their stunning, raw silk, fuchsia suit, feeling a little ridiculous to be driving our old camper. I was wired and worried and kept reminding myself to stay centered as I rode the elevator up the 74 stories to the penthouse restaurant club. The setting for this talk felt especially intimidating. I had to wait during the entire fashion show, and that meant a lot of deep breathing. The moment of panic came when I glanced down at my lap and almost fainted. My skirt was covered with black specks! The exhaust from the camper must have sprayed me. I panicked. What could I do? I resolved to appear confident and calm. Maybe no one would notice. And in any case, what could I do at that point?

At last the moderator wound up her seemingly endless fashion show and introduced me. I felt as though I had to struggle against the tide the whole time, but I got through the talk and even received positive feedback. (See, you really can trust yourself to do it, even when you are as distracted and dismayed as I was.) Can you guess the end to this story? That afternoon, I rushed straight to my favorite dry cleaner. I anxiously awaited their pronouncement. How could I ever afford to replace this costly suit? I was embarrassed, again, when they told me the verdict. The specks had always been there. They were part of the raw silk's natural imperfections. In my altered, prespeech state, those black specks had been magnified tenfold. That's the last time I will ever wear someone else's garment.

Be Audience-Centered

It's a bit of a juggling act to attend closely to your dress and monitor your behavior without becoming overly preoccupied with yourself. Yet self-consciousness inhibits dynamic delivery, and if you focus exclusively on yourself, you become susceptible. The best way to escape self-consciousness is to focus on the audience. Remember that you are there to serve *them*. Without them, there would be no presentation. Although your behavior is important, you are really "just" a messenger. If you think in these terms, the primary question becomes not "How am I doing?" but "How are *they* doing?" Think of yourself as that gracious hostess, seeking to ensure your guests' comfort and pleasure.

Take advantage of the two-way nature of eye contact. What do you see? Are they listening? Are they awake? Adjust your content as well as your pace accordingly. If they look tired because the meeting has gone on longer than expected, don't talk faster, talk less. If a snowstorm has started and people keep glancing out the window, relieve their anxiety by reassuring them you'll end early if conditions do not let up. However tempting it may be to "seize the day," remind yourself that your listeners won't be able to absorb your message if they are distracted. When something happens that is beyond your control, let go. Your success is guaranteed when your interest and concern for the audience is transparent and sincere.

I have also learned not to be distracted by the one or two participants who may look askance throughout the entire presentation. When I first started speaking, if I saw a furrowed brow, I worried all the time, sure that the listener hated and berated everything I said. So at the break I would go over to see how she was doing and whether I could answer any questions.

Time after time, it would turn out that my tormentor was, in fact, enraptured by my talk—fully absorbed and wildly enthusiastic. The look I mistook for judgment and rejection turned out to be an expression of intense concentration. Now, I don't get distracted by one or two frowners. On the other hand, if almost everyone in the room has her brow furrowed, there might be a problem.

Check it out! You gain valuable information from the audience. Are they expecting a lunch break when you announce that you will spend the next half hour reviewing the current crisis? Has an official stepped into the door behind you, worriedly searching the audience? Have the five fire trucks that stopped just down the street made everyone obviously long to go to the window? You can adapt to these situations. Invite and investigate your audience's reactions so that you can make use of what you learn.

LET YOUR SPEECH REFLECT YOUR CONFIDENCE

This would be a good place to talk about the image we project with our feminine style of speech. While many aspects of women's traditional collaborative speaking style are positive strengths, there are various ways in which women undercut themselves in everyday speech, as well as in presentations. Robin Lakoff observed that many women are reared under the influence of unspoken "Rules of Rapport" for women: "Don't Impose, Give Options, and Be Friendly." This heritage often leads us to use an indirect style of speaking strewn with "hedges" (sort of, kind of), qualifiers (just a, little), intensifiers (really, so, very), and tag questions (isn't it? don't you?). Spurred by our traditional conditioning, we weaken the force of opinions and feelings all the more by adding comments that are self-deprecatory and apologetic, just in case someone may be offended by what we say. Women just might feel kind of uncomfortable putting someone in what they may feel was sort of a really tough spot, don't you think?

From the perspective of many male listeners, such statements become too vague and mired in excessive verbiage for the message to penetrate. Even the use of intensifiers serves to undermine, rather than strengthen the message: "I think that's *such* a good idea. I *really* want to do that," can be perceived as weaker than "That's a good idea; I'll do it."

Especially in mixed groups, the feminine style tends toward disclaimers and apologies: "I'm not absolutely certain, but . . ."; "I'm sorry to bother you, but . . ."; "You probably aren't interested. . . ."; "I'm not a very good speaker, but . . ."; "You've probably already thought of this. . . ." We offer these remarks with a tilt of the head, a shrug of the shoulders, a smile, or even a giggle in order to smooth the conversation, facilitate a dialogue, put the listeners at ease, and empower them. But we would be wise to take note that in the eyes of many people, and especially of men, such language puts us in a lower position on the hierarchy of confidence and credibility.

For example, imagine that I am at a meeting of master gardeners, and I am demonstrating how to care for roses. I feel well prepared, confident, and competent. But because it is my habit as a woman, I may make a mildly deprecatory remark about my pruning skills in order to help the newcomer feel at ease. If the newcomer is female, she will follow the unspoken ritual by responding with a compliment on how masterfully I've demonstrated the technique. If the newcomer is male, he may hear my remark as a lack of confidence or even competence. Instead of responding with the expected compliment, he may silently resolve to give my talents less credibility; he may take the interchange as an opportunity to display his own talents or even as an opening to teach me something he thinks, based on my remarks, I don't know.

Women make frequent use of tag questions to foster consensus. "That was a great movie, wasn't it?" Men also use tags, but typically to reinforce their message. "We'll be home by eight, won't we!" The feminine speaking style also utilizes a great deal of rising inflection at the end of declarative sentences, as a strategy to soften direct statements. Some listeners will hear this not as diplomacy, but as indecisiveness, questioning, and uncertainty.

The use of "I'm sorry" presents an interesting example of cross-gender miscommunication. Women's speech is often littered with this expression, though we're not apologizing or assuming guilt or causality. Rather, we're using it to show our empathy or concern, to establish a connection with others. We expect the other person to reciprocate and not take the "I'm sorry" literally. But it is only effective if it is mutually understood. When my husband told me that the Sonics lost the playoff game, he looked at me as if I were crazy when I said, "I'm so sorry." My friend Aniko recalls one day when she sympathetically clucked how sorry she was to a male friend who told her how he'd run out of gas. He replied, "That's okay, it's not your fault." His assuming this one-up position was irksome and left her feeling one-down. She expected a warm response, like "Thanks, it was a rough day."

It is not clear whether women speakers increase their ability to influence and be taken seriously when they delete the qualifiers and disclaimers, edit their speech to be more concise, and reframe their requests to be more direct. Indeed, because there is a social *expectation* that we will speak tentatively and indirectly, we often find ourselves in a very difficult double bind. While we may not be taken seriously if we embrace the noncompetitive, accommodating style, we might be called strident or bossy if we try to be more assertive. Consider the dilemma of Hillary Rodham Clinton. In the first years of the Clinton administration, she was castigated for being "careerist." Dignitaries bragged about calling her by her first name, yet scorned her for calling senators by their first names. Jokes and derogatory remarks about her abounded. As Robin Lakoff puts it, ". . . when a woman is placed in a position in which being assertive and forceful is necessary, she is faced with a paradox: she can be a good woman but a bad executive or professional; or vice versa. To do both is impossible."

There are no easy answers to resolve this dilemma. According to studies by psychologist Linda Carli, when women speak tentatively, they are more influential with men but less influential with women. This is substantiated by the observations of sociologist Carol Tavris: "Even though the men regarded an assertive woman as being more knowledgeable and competent than a woman who said the same thing but with hesitations, they were more influenced by a woman who spoke tentatively. They liked her more and found her more trustworthy."

And what about same-gender interactions? I often find that my indirect requests work splendidly with many of my women friends, but are not effective with my husband. When I say "Ugh, it's really feeling stuffy and hot," he does not seize the initiative to open the window. I am working on making a direct request, "Please open the window." Yet changing style is not as simple as it may sound. When I adapt my style, my gut persists in telling me I'm being too directive and bossy and "not nice."

All this is discouraging because if we persist in playing by feminine rules, we will be seen as ineffectual and remain unable to become authoritative or powerful catalysts for change. If we choose the path of assimilation, we perpetuate the exclusive use of masculine speaking styles and neglect to change hierarchical institutes, while implicitly condoning the notion that women who aspire to high positions are "uppity."

As we become aware of the double bind, we *can* change.

We can be more direct and still be good listeners. We can save our smiles for the positive moments and hold our gaze steady for the heavy ones. We can continue to hold our basic feminine style in high esteem, while at the same time eliminating qualifiers that make us appear tentative. Best of all, we can contribute our facilitative people skills as speakers, even while realizing that in many situations, for our message to be heard, we have to overcome our conditioning and learn to speak more directly.

TIPS FOR SPEAKING WITH POWER AND POISE

Here is a chart of the pointers we have discussed to help you review:

YES! Do more of this:	NO! Avoid this:
Body	
eye contact	looking at ceiling or floor, rolling or closing eyes
animated face	deadpan expression
warm smile	scowl or grimace
relaxed body	clenched fists, locked elbows, clasped hands
meaningful, dynamic gestures	fidgeting or toying
strong, tall posture	hunching or slumping
weight on both feet	shifting the hips, rocking, tapping the foot
full use of space; approach audience	clutching podium or standing in one spot
professional dress	sloppy or inappropriate attire

Voice

vocal energy through volume	too soft
breathing through to the last syllable	fading at ends of phrases
varied and expressive	singsong or monotone
clear and well enunciated	mumbling
relaxed and resonant	shrill or excessively high-pitched
well-paced, frequent pauses	rushed or labored pace

Behavior

bold, confident appearance	nervous laugh, shrugging shoulders
graceful recovery; humor	apologizing, sighing, rolling eyes, defensiveness
spontaneous; responsive to audience	wed to text; reading a script
personal	overly formal and abstract
confident and direct	qualifiers (sorta, kinda), fillers (you know, um)
original and creative	clichés and slang
brevity; short sentences	exceeding time limit; complex sentences

Speak from your heart to their eyes. If you present yourself with enthusiasm and energy, the audience will respond. As you may recall from the last chapter's discussion on voice, I think of myself as the battery that supplies the juice for each listener's attention. I need to plug into each member of the audience. The more people there are, the more juice I need, so I crank up my energy and produce greater volume, larger gestures, and more dramatic pauses. I have been delighted and surprised to find that this energizing current runs two ways.

That is, my listeners' interest, laughter, and applause feed *my* energy. And the larger the audience, the more energy I receive. Believe it or not, I have come to look forward to those rare chances to speak to groups with more than seventy-five audience members. An audience of several hundred becomes positively electrifying! While the butterfly count of nervous anticipation multiplies exponentially, I know that I can depend on mental training strategies and careful preparation to carry me, and the tremendous high I get from speaking to a large crowd makes it all worthwhile. You can do it, too!

Remember, different speakers have different styles. Some are quite reserved, others are very expressive. Find and enjoy your own style. You wouldn't expect a speech by Hillary Clinton to look or sound like one by Oprah Winfrey, but both are effective. The magic ingredient that will ignite your delivery is your vitality, your caring, and your energy. Release them, and you will be irresistible.

A TOOLBOX FOR EVERYDAY SPEAKING

With planning you can reinforce your message by using visual aids and a range of techniques.

How can we hold an audience's attention in this epoch of instant and global videography, computerized sound tracks, and
multiple images? With the advent of TV, people have become
accustomed to processing many visual and auditory images
and signals at once in short, rapidly changing bursts. Click!
Zap! Whiz! With remote control in hand, that's how quickly
people can tune out, switch stations, and fast-forward if the
subject on the screen starts to bore them. While trying to pay
attention to us in a live setting, our listeners can't literally zap
us, but they can do it mentally if they become frustrated by too
slow a pace or not enough visual stimulation. We need a toolbox packed with tricks to enhance our presentation and engage our audience that is built on updated knowledge of listening habits, the various media we can use, and the way the
environment affects our audience.

I became aware of how the media age affects our attention
when my children were small and we watched "Sesame
Street" together. I objected to the rapid-fire style of the show. I
felt it encouraged the development of short attention spans, in-
hibiting children's ability to stick with a subject for more than
a minute or two. I preferred the more laid-back, in-depth pace
of "Mr. Rogers." Happily, my children enjoyed both. And now
I understand that "Sesame Street" was preparing them for

their world of 233 MHz processors with MMX technology requiring 64 MB of RAM. Yet I also recognize that "Mr. Rogers" satisfied the human yearning for relationship and depth of meaning. As speakers, we should keep both styles of information presentation in mind.

We do need to adapt and vary our pace to keep our listeners from pushing that mental button that tunes us out. We need to speak in short, direct, and vivid phrases; move around; and transition to a new "scene" or key idea every five minutes or so. We need to use a variety of visual aids to improve the chance that our presentation will be remembered. Yet even with these adaptations to the modern world of high technology, we can rest assured that there is still a place for the qualities "Mr. Rogers" champions. People will always appreciate the warm atmosphere created by a real, live, personal presenter who looks them straight in the eye and respects their intelligence. It's just that they will appreciate us more if we can keep pace with their capacity to register information on multiple "channels."

BROADCAST ON ALL CHANNELS: VISUAL, AUDITORY, KINESTHETIC

We take in and process information primarily through the senses of sight and sound, and through kinesthesia, which detects position or movement of the body. Each of us has a *preferred* channel or modality, although most favor a blend of two or even three. Which is your strongest mode? Consider how you like to get directions to someone's house. Are you a *visual* learner who wants a map with landmarks clearly labeled? Or do you want to *hear* how to get there, including street names and distances? Or perhaps you respond best to *kinesthetic* instruction, preferring someone to just point you in the right direction.

Those who are predominantly visual want to see an overview first. They respond to metaphors and analogies and prefer pictures. Auditory learners process information best by hearing details, statistics, and facts in a clear and organized fashion, with each step clearly explained. And kinesthetic types learn by doing and by feeling. They like opportunities to interact, to discuss, and to participate in hands-on activities.

In a group situation, we need to broadcast on all three channels, which takes some thought and care, as we tend to be most comfortable in our own modality. In Chapter 4 we talked about organizing and presenting information to build in variety and balance. Let's take it a step farther and see how we can incorporate a variety of activities.

Let's take the case of designing a presentation for your book group. Imagine that you're feeling a bit bored with recent selections and hope the group will take on a new focus by reading a range of international women authors, thereby gaining some insights into different parts of the world. After reading this chapter, you decide to take a little time to prepare so that you will get the group excited and committed to a new plan. As a way of appealing to all learning styles, you might include the following devices in your informal presentation:

• **Show a map:** Display a world map and ask group members to mark the countries where they have connections—through travel, study, or relationships. Visual learners like the picture, kinesthetics enjoy putting their mark on it, auditories are pleased with the details and facts.

• **Elicit a list:** Guide your friends in brainstorming all the women authors they can think of from different parts of the world. List them on sticky notes, and place them on the map. Kinesthetics like the participation, visuals get the picture, auditories feel comfortable talking about and hearing the details unfold while having them displayed.

• **Show a picture:** Display the picture of the author on the back cover of *Nervous Conditions* by Tsitsi Dangarembga, which is the kind of book you hope the group will begin to read. Give a brief biography of the author, and express the sense of heightened understanding that came from your reading this book. Kinesthetics will feel your enthusiasm, auditories will appreciate hearing the details, visuals will like the picture.

• **Tell a story:** Tell a story from *Nervous Conditions*. Share the scene where the young girl travels out of her tiny village for the first time and sees her new school. Express her wonder at flowers planted simply for beauty, not for food. Kinesthetics will respond to the emotion, visuals will gain a picture of the time and place of the novel, auditories will respond to your expressive voice.

• **Hand out a list and pass around several books:** Distribute the list of books you obtained from the library and pass around several suggested books. Auditories like the details, visuals can examine the book covers, kinesthetics can leaf through the books.

• **Assign continents:** Describe your proposal for each member to take on a continent and come in with background information, suggested readings, representative refreshments, and music. Refer back to the map and ask for volunteers. Kinesthetics will like the hands-on approach, visuals will respond to the big picture, and auditories will appreciate the organization and facts to come.

There is yet another channel that is universal for all audiences members: the gustatory channel! You may want to provide refreshments. It's amazing how an inexpensive bag of candy can perk up your listeners. Just the visual stimulation of seeing candy kisses on the table seems to enhance attention.

VARY THE PACE

In addition to appealing to a wider range of appetites, broad-casting on all channels also adds variety. Remember how our mind dismisses repetitive input as irrelevant background noise. Attention is reserved for the new and innovative, which means that variety is ever important. Here are some other ways to vary the pace:

• **Stretch breaks:** Stretching is valuable during a presentation, even for just a minute or two. People don't leave the room but feel free to stand in place, chat, stretch. Help them along by doing your own stretches. A short break noticeably generates new energy.

• **Buzz groups:** If eyes seem to be glazing over, create a way to draw people out of the passive listening mode. Ask them to speak to a person sitting nearby for a few minutes about something related to your topic.

• **Creative movement:** Build in an activity where people actually get up and move around while still working on the topic. Give them an interview sheet that requires them to meet a range of people. Have them count off by the number of tables and move to new seats. Send them off in small groups with a short and defined assignment.

• **Fun and games:** Incorporate activities such as role-plays, simulations, and games to increase involvement and inject fun. Write relevant questions or quotes on note cards and tape them under a few chairs; then invite the audience to find and share them. I love to prowl toy stores to find amusing things to use in games and role-plays—koosh balls, rubber chickens, stuffed animals, play money, magic wands.

LEAVEN WITH LAUGHTER

Humor offers another way to vary the pace and mood of any presentation. It puts the listener at ease and builds receptivity to you and your message; and it relaxes you. Inject natural humor in your style. This does not mean joke telling, unless that's your forte, and even then it would be wise to proceed with caution. When you tell a joke, you have to be sure it is not offensive to any participant, is relevant to the topic, and is not stale. The audience will resent contrived jokes that are unrelated to your subject. With contemporary sensitivity to diversity issues, old-fashioned jokes are too often offensive. If you are uncertain how something will go over or whether it may be received as insensitive, delete it! Dig for more creativity to find fresh and spontaneous sources of humor. Make sure it's the right time and place for humor. If you find yourself carried away and say something that might offend someone, apologize.

People tend to assume that a great sense of humor, like good speaking skills, must be an inborn gift. Yet both are talents that can be cultivated. Listen to tapes of your favorite comic, buy collections of your favorite comic strips, and keep a notebook of funny lines and stories. Learn to play with the three key elements of humor: repetition, exaggeration and surprise. Use poetic license to make a story funnier and more personal by putting yourself in it. Soon you will find that your worst predicaments are your best sources of humor. My family often tells funny stories from the week at the dinner table. It's a great stress reducer. Now, when something seemingly terrible happens, I find myself saying, "Whoa! They'll never believe this. It'll make a great story. I can't wait to tell the family about this one," instead of, "How awful, I can't believe this is happening to me."

For the visual learners in your group, cut out relevant cartoons or photographs that illustrate your message in a funny way, and display them on an overhead projector (for a large group) or pass them around the room. Auditories will love limericks and rhymes. For the kinesthetics, mime or role-playing a funny situation that helps make your point will be sure to please the players and the watchers. A word of warning, however: Never drag a reluctant participant into a role-play. Ask for volunteers. Those who come forward are most certainly your extroverted kinesthetic learners.

Fit relevant hunks of humor into your message, but remember that the message is primary. Don't force it. Work on your timing. A slight pause gives the audience a chance to respond. Get the laughs when you can, but don't wait for long. Just keep going if the laughter never comes.

CREATE THE AMBIENCE YOU WANT

The physical environment is part of your speech. The setting influences the mood in the room, the tone of your remarks, and the response you get, and it either promotes or inhibits the listeners' ability to attend, absorb, and appreciate your talk. If audience members are uncomfortable or can't see or hear you, they will focus on seeking relief for their discomfort and not on your words, no matter how wise, witty, or wonderful they may be. If something about the room makes you feel awkward—if the lighting is insufficient or too bright and harsh, for example—you will struggle with this invisible foe the whole time. Artful management of these elements has been refined by the Chinese into an ancient practice called *feng shui*, which is devoted to enhancing ambience and the flow of energy. You may want to bring flowers or art objects to provide an attractive or inspirational focal point. Consider displaying relevant posters, flags, or banners. Enhancing the environment is important in making your presentation successful.

Assess the Space

When looking at the room where you will be speaking, consider the following:

- How is the room set up?
- What will be the size of the audience?
- Will there be adequate seating?
- Where will the speakers stand or sit?
- Is the equipment for visual aids in place?
- Is the lighting appropriate?
- Is there adequate ventilation?
- Is there adequate amplification?

Beginning speakers often see problems ahead of time but don't feel comfortable asking for changes. Yet you have every right to ask and to make the changes yourself, if need be. You need the sensitivity and skill of a stage manager to handle all the details of props, logistics, timing, and placement.

Take the time and invest the effort to make the room setup work for you. If the furniture isn't bolted to the ground, you will probably want to move it. This is true whether it's a small, informal gathering like your book group at your home, or a symposium in the ballroom of a downtown hotel. The seating arrangement creates a flow of energy and a relationship to you as the speaker. Even introducing just a slight curve to the theater-style rows in a room can shift that flow and create a friendly, more responsive atmosphere. Don't be shy about rearranging the furniture. The fuss you make at the beginning of any meeting is well worth the bother.

Let's consider those informal gatherings and meetings. Simply by rearranging your living room furniture to create a *circle* for the group, you will enhance relationships and maximize participation. Circles are powerful equalizers, and they allow eye contact among all members of a group. The group dynamic cannot develop as successfully if some of the participants are blocked from view of the others or are in a back-row position.

Large meeting rooms for more formal situations can be set up in one of several ways. Each of the following suggestions includes the psychological effect you can expect the arrangement to have on the participants:

• **Theater or auditorium style:** The audience is clearly in a passive mode, prepared to sit back, be enlightened, entertained, or informed, and take in the presentation with minimal participation.

• **Classroom style:** The listeners are seated, again, in rows, but this time at tables. The relationship between speaker and audience becomes a teacher-student one. There is a power imbalance, and the implied message is that the speaker has the answers and the information. The group members are to listen, take notes, and perhaps ask questions, but they get the message that they are to participate only minimally. If the rows are angled slightly, in a curve or herringbone pattern, the participants will relate better to one another.

• **Horseshoe style:** The audience will relate to each other as well as to the speaker, and the speaker can get closer to the audience. Audience members will feel that their participation, through interaction and discussion, is being encouraged.

• **Conference style:** The size and shape of the table has an impact. A rectangular table with the speaker seated at one end gives the speaker an aura of influence that is greater than that of the rest of the group. Participants sit on opposite sides of the table alongside their like-minded friends. An atmosphere of "us" versus "them" might arise if the subject is controversial. A round table, on the other hand, puts everyone on a level playing field. Everyone is visible; everyone feels included.

• **Cloverleaf style:** People are sometimes grouped at small tables, where they have a strong relationship to their subgroup cluster, as well as to the other clusters in the room, with the presenter up front in the "stem." This configuration works well for a workshop setting, where you want people to work in break-out groups.

Control the Atmosphere

The *size* of the room also has a powerful influence on the atmosphere and comfort of the audience. If your gathering is small and the room is large, the empty space seems to absorb the energy you send out into the room. It's better to work in a room that is a bit crowded. It gives a cozy feeling and sends the message that this is a popular, important event. If the room is larger than needed, and you can't do anything about it, insist that the participants gather close together so that you can feel like a group. Remove extra chairs or tables to eliminate the feeling that the empty chairs represent people who did not come. You can place "reserved" signs on back rows or tables to help direct people to the front as they enter, and then remove the signs as additional space is needed. If you had planned to stand before a large group, and your audience turns out to be small, you might consider forming a circle or semi-circle of chairs at the last minute so that all participants have their backs to the empty spaces in the room.

How will you handle the opposite problem, when the room overflows with people? If you expect more people than the room has been prepared to hold, find out beforehand where you can gain access to extra chairs. Set the room up so late-comers will come in at the back. It will be disruptive and distracting for you and the audience if someone has to slink by the podium, not to mention how the poor latecomer will feel. It is always best to anticipate the need for such measures to prevent problems once your program begins.

When you call a meeting, you need to attend to the environment outside of the room. You will need to be sure guests have good directions, plenty of room to park, and supplies in the bathrooms, even if the gathering is not in your house but at a school building or community center. Is the appointed room clearly marked so that people won't get lost in a large building? Is coffee, or at least water, available? Where do coats and umbrellas go? How will guests be greeted? Consider using name tags or a guest register. Attention to all of these details will ensure that the audience and presenters are in the best possible frame of mind for a successful event. Even when you are an invited guest at a speaking engagement, it is wise to delve into these concerns since the comfort of the audience ultimately determines the effective delivery of your message.

Whether you are the speaker, the introducer, the chair, or a panelist, circulate among the guests as they arrive. Build allies and familiarity. This will help put you and the guests at ease and will help energize you as you begin speaking. This kind of preparation breeds confidence, poise, and power.

Before launching into your speech, check in with your audience. They'll appreciate it when you inquire, "Is everyone comfortable?" "Do you want the door closed or the shades drawn?" Of course, don't inquire about aspects you can't change. It's frustrating to be in a stuffy room and have the presenter comment on the heat although she has no remedy to offer. Let the participants know when breaks are planned and where the facilities are located. Tell them about designated smoking areas, where can they get water or coffee, and where and when they can use the rest rooms and phones.

Decide on the Speaker's Place

Tradition places formal speakers up on a platform and behind a lectern. But the authority and power such placement is meant to convey do not play well with audiences these days. Relationship building and direct interaction are the keys to a successful speaking engagement, whether the goal is to persuade, influence, or inspire, and the barrier the podium and stage create interferes with the speaker's relationship to the audience. With lavaliere microphones, there is no longer any need to stay at a lectern. In Chapter 8, in the section on movement, we contrasted the formal style of the original Nixon/Kennedy debates of 1960 with the presidential debates of 1996, when Bob Dole and Bill Clinton sat perched on stools on a small stage in the center of an intimate audience— cabaret style. They got up and moved around. The message is clear. "Up close and personal" is the order of the day.

I like to have a small table at the front of the room where I can set up my notes and any props I have brought with me, yet still have ample space to move around in. Take special care setting up this front area, which is where you will begin and end your talk. Make sure there is enough room for you to get past any furniture or fixtures so that you can move freely and approach the audience at a comfortable distance. I recall a presentation when I neglected this important point. During the entire time, I felt trapped in a narrow space between the overhead projector and a table. Somehow, once I started talking, the momentum swept me away and left me feeling helpless to change anything. The main message, again, is *take charge!* Be proactive in creating the atmosphere conducive to your objectives, whether they be social, professional, organizational, or educational.

It is a good idea to have a pen available to jot notes or adjust time frames on your note cards. Make sure a pitcher of water and sturdy glass are set up for your use. Beware of flimsy plastic cups. When you are flying high with the energy of a presentation, your fine motor skills may desert you, and your hand may not take kindly to executing refined movements. In fact, I prefer to bring my own water bottle, because I trust I can take a delicate sip from the straw. Check the floor where you will be moving. Use duct tape to fasten down any cords that might trip you.

To be proactive in these considerations of space and setup, discuss your needs early on with your hosts. For those more formal situations when you may be addressing an audience in a public space, work closely with the people setting up the event, such as the sponsoring group and the hotel or conference facility staff. An important lesson I have had to learn and relearn is *assume nothing!* Double-check everything! The people you are checking with may not have experience or expertise. They may not have thought about the things that will concern you, so ask a lot of questions, specify what you want, fax each other sketches, and reconfirm arrangements as the day grows nearer. Talk directly to the facilities manager. Go to the facility the day before, if possible, and inspect the setup. Arrive as early as possible to allow time for troubleshooting. Miscommunication and missing elements are inevitable. So build in time for fixing any glitches.

Adjust the Sound and Light

Sound and light are part of the environment. Try to have the room as well lit as possible. Could extra halogen floor lamps be brought in? Curtains opened? Avoid standing in front of a brightly lit window, as it will be hard on the audience's eyes and will make you look like a shadow puppet. On the other hand, if there is a large window behind the audience, you might find the glare distracting or even headache-inducing. Are shades available to keep the sun from glaring in or to screen out visual distractions?

How will the room be darkened if you show slides or other visual aids? Is it possible to cover the windows? Check ahead, so that if it is not possible, you can request a different room, or at least select visual aids that will not require a darkened room. Where are the light switches? It's frustrating and anticlimactic if you get trapped into the confusion of looking for the switch when the group is primed and ready for your visual aids.

What is the sound environment like? How can you eliminate distracting background noise like air conditioners, fans, street traffic, and people talking in the hallway? Check with your contact person to find out what else is afoot on the day of your program, and prompt her to consider what makes good neighbors. I remember one session where there was a choir practicing on the other side of the flimsy divider. Their music was outstanding—and thunderous—drowning out my words. Is there background music pumped into this space? How can it be turned off? One gathering left my voice raw after talking over the noisy Coke machine for an hour.

What about room temperature and ventilation? Is the room unusually hot or cold? Do you have any control over that? Thermostat? Windows? Shades? Remember, the presence of many bodies will raise the temperature, so start off with a cool room. It's better to have people a bit chilled than toasty-warm and lulled into a siesta during your talk. As always, be creative. In anticipation of the intense heat at an annual July session I facilitate, the invitation includes a call to BYOFF, "Bring Your Own Floor Fan." We'd never make it through the program without our collaboratively created breeze.

Make Friends with the Microphone

Whenever possible, I speak without one, but microphones are often necessary. You are wise to talk to the facilities person ahead of time to see what kind of microphone is available. A stationary mike allows your hands to be free, but keeps you wedded to one spot. A handheld mike allows you to move around, but ties up a hand and keeps you dodging the cord. A lavaliere mike allows you to move around and have your hands free, although you still have to deal with the cord.

The best of all possibilities is the wireless lavaliere—no cord, free hands, full mobility. But it's not without a few challenges. First, the standard equipment is designed to work easily with men's suits and ties. A soft silk blouse will not look right with the heavy mike weighing down one side. It is possible to have a medallion-style arrangement, where the mike hangs from a cord. Clearly this is the best choice for most feminine apparel unless you wear a jacket, but not all facilities have this type. And the medallion wireless mikes still require use of a small transmitter unit, about the size of a beeper, that must be clipped to something—a belt or sturdy pocket. There are some excellent, modestly priced portable units that your organization may want to invest in. Communication is the lifeblood of any group, and you have to be heard over the crowd to connect.

Another challenge that wireless units present is the possibility of a "no walk zone": If you go beyond a certain boundary, a horrible shriek of feedback may assault your group, or there may be dead spots where something blocks the signal. On the other hand, some wireless mikes are powerful enough transmitters so that if you walk out of the room and forget to turn them off, your audience can hear you wherever you go. The potential for embarrassment in this situation is high, indeed. My editor remembers a workshop where the facilitator walked into the hallway at the start of a break, and all the participants heard him over the loudspeaker propositioning the event's lovely coordinator! (She refused.) If you are using such a mike, watch what you say, and turn off the power!

Jewelry creates another problem for a lavaliere mike. I recall a Sunday school banquet where I was decked out in my pearls. As I launched into my talk on motivating and retaining volunteers, I was dismayed to hear loud, distracting thunks. I finally realized they were emanating from my necklace, as the slightest movement jostled it against the mike. I recovered by removing the pearls while talking about the need to treat volunteers gently, like a fine strand of pearls, thus threading the necklace into my talk. Humor and imagery help, but since then I've learned to plan what I wear with these equipment requirements in mind.

There are different kinds of microphones, and they vary in sensitivity, so be sure to try out each one before the audience arrives. Practice lowering and raising a stationary mike so that you can do it smoothly. Find out how to switch the mike off if you need to cough or sneeze. Test out its responsiveness. Some have a very narrow range, so if you turn your head, the mike misses your words. With these, your mouth should be about eight to twelve inches away. Look at the audience on either side by tilting your head but keeping your mouth in line with the mike. With a handheld mike, remember to move the mike as you move your head so that you can keep your mouth in line with it at a steady distance. Watch out for getting so close to the mike that your P's pop or S's hiss. Test the sound levels: too soft and the group will strain and tire and tune out; too loud and they'll wince and shut down to protect their ears. Squeals of feedback may indicate that the volume is too high or the speakers too close to the microphone.

When it is impossible to check this all out ahead of time,

take a moment before you launch into your topic. Adjust the height of a stationary mike before you begin speaking—don't lean over or stand on tiptoes. Check the sound level, not by blowing into the mike or tapping it, just by counting in a normal tone, "testing, one, two, three." Ask various sectors of the audience to raise their hands if they can hear you comfortably.

Speak to the audience, not the mike. Apply what you learned for speaking into the telephone receiver, and send your voice *through* the microphone, rather than stopping at it, so that the tone comes through with energy and clarity, rather than muffled and dull. The mike provides the amplification, but only *you* can provide the energy and animation. The only element the mike changes is volume—you don't have to tire yourself by overprojecting, but you do still have to project your voice with verve.

MASTERMIND THE PROGRAM

Sometimes your concern must go beyond the room setup to embrace the whole design of the event or meeting. Recently I came across an invitation to a Martin Luther King Day breakfast meeting for the African American Jewish Coalition for Justice. I was interested in joining this group and considered attending the breakfast. My interest was to connect and interact with other members, not just listen to a speaker, even though he was an interesting one. I called to inquire what their goals were for the gathering. The organizers hadn't really thought about it. They had planned the breakfast, reserved the date, invited the speaker, and assumed they were set.

I suggested they build into the program some opportunity for structured sharing among those attending since, as we explored the issue, they came to realize that their ultimate goal was to build membership and fellowship. I was delighted when they asked if I would help design an activity. We shortened the length of the speaker's talk, and I spoke with him at length to help him discover ways to link his talk into the group's overall goals and purpose. Then we devoted half of the session to interaction. We asked people to break into small groups and share what Martin Luther King meant to them personally, and then we had each group report on some of their experiences with the whole gathering. The sharing generated new relationships, excitement, and commitment to the organization. We closed by joining in a circle (yes, we had to push chairs and tables around), holding hands, and singing.

It may sound corny, but the emotion and inspiration were palpable. I believe any group event benefits by involving the participants in a structured process that helps them interact. In this age of high tech, the personal touch offers a needed counterbalance. Think of a glitzy multimedia show where you sit passively and awkwardly next to others, then leave without interacting or getting to know anyone. Now contrast it to a highly interactive session where you share experiences and interact positively with a small group, exchanging phone numbers and resources with others.

We are creatures of habit who don't realize we can approach an event this way. Let's remember to question everything! Next time you are part of a planning group, invited to speak, or, as in my case, just planning to attend, consider options beyond simply having a speaker. Ask yourself, what is the vision or mission of the group and this particular event? Play with the design of the whole event to find the best way to fulfill that vision. With forethought, you can turn everyday meetings and events into opportunities for positive transformation.

MAKE NOTES TO KEEP YOU ON TRACK

You learned in Chapter 4 that notes can serve as an itinerary to keep you on a direct route and on time for each destination. A carefully prepared set of note cards will boost your poise and confidence. How speakers go about making notes is as individual as their personalities. I prefer 4 × 6 index cards because I like their stiffness. They are easy to hold and maneuver and don't rattle like thinner paper. I print my notes large enough so that I can read them at a glance. I use different colors to cue me when to introduce visual aids, handouts, or exercises. I start a new card for each subtopic, and I write only the key words that will help me make transitions, along with quotations and statistics.

Sometimes pictures and symbols are better than words. They don't have to be pretty or even identifiable to anyone but yourself. Pictures are more easily remembered than words, and they can convey more dense, complex relationships, so at a glance you can find your place and jog your memory. For example, when I present the Maslow hierarchy of motivating needs, discussed in Chapter 6, I draw the pyramid and refer to it. Sprinkle your notes with arrows and numbers, and enjoy the creative process.

Timing Is Everything

One way I use my index cards is to mark prominently the time I intend to spend on each section of my talk. This helps me do any necessary editing *within* my presentation, preventing me from getting to the end of the time and realizing that I have presented only a fraction of what I had planned. If I have control over the start time, I write a target beginning time for each segment of my presentation, in increments as small as two and three minutes for a short talk. If I don't have control, or if the time is likely to get off schedule, I just note the number of minutes it takes for each segment. I set up my small, digital clock, which is also a stopwatch, and start the timer when I begin to track the total number of minutes. (It's surprising how many meeting rooms are without reliable, visible clocks.)

The most important aspect of timing is to note when to begin your closing—to reserve ample time so that you can end firmly, graciously, and with power and poise. Be sure to end on time or, better yet, end early. Just because you have been allotted 45 minutes doesn't mean you have to use the whole time. If you appear late in the program, be prepared to do some on-the-spot editing. Early speakers often go over their time allotment, and the program gets behind schedule. This means you must plan for 20-, 25-, and even 10-minute versions of your talk.

If you are speaking just before a break that will involve food, audience attention is focused on the anticipation of refreshments. During or after lunch, people may be concerned about getting back to work and their bodies are busy digesting, so keep your remarks short and lively. At dinner meetings, there are likely to be the additional challenges brought on by fatigue, subdued lighting, pre-dinner cocktails, full stomachs, and dinner wine. For such situations, when ending early is the right thing to do, I try to be prepared with a shortened version of my talk.

If you see that the situation warrants it, you may even want to reveal ahead of time your plan to end early. The audience will relax and be more receptive. Remember that almost any group today is conditioned for the commercial break at ten-minute intervals, and many of their favorite programs are only a half hour long.

If there are several speakers on a program, get an early spot.

I remember my experience in the "spotted" silk fuschia suit at the fashion show. My agony was prolonged by the extended delay. The moderator kept bringing on more models while I watched my time allotment shrink and my anxiety expand. The fashion show ended twenty minutes late. I was left with the dilemma of cutting my presentation in half or having half the audience more than likely exit during my talk to get back to their workday on time. What a lesson! Now I know to request being first on any program.

Just be certain that the following phrases NEVER find their way into your notes or across your lips: "*I wish I had more time . . . I may not finish. . . . We may have to go over our allotted time . . . I am halfway through my talk but I've only covered a fourth of the materials. . . .*" Such phrases cause your listeners to feel tense, distracted, and betrayed. If you don't tell them what they're missing, they'll never know.

DON'T READ A BEDTIME STORY

What if you decide to read from a text? I can think of many occasions when you may want to read a poem or excerpts from a journal, a book, or someone else's speech. Perhaps you will be asked to read the life history of the deceased at a memorial service. Beware! It is harder to be effective while reading a text than when speaking extemporaneously. Without careful preparation and practice, you can lose vitality and bore your listeners to the extent that they mentally pick up that dreaded "remote control."

It's best to limit the amount of reading you do in a presentation. But when it is appropriate to read, go over the material enough before the presentation so that you don't have to give up the eye contact that is essential to keeping your audience's attention. Mark the text in places where you will pause, and remember to keep an appropriate pace. Almost everyone speeds up when reading aloud, which results in less precise articulation and projection. Resist this impulse. Slow down and remember to pause generously. Adapt the text with your delivery in mind, perhaps making the language more direct and interactive than it is in its written form. For example, when a sentence is written in the passive voice, you can easily make it more dynamic by converting to the active voice. Instead of "Danaan will be remembered as a peacemaker," try "We will remember Danaan as a peacemaker." Instead of "There is a second point to consider," try, "Now let's look at the second point."

Think of the text as a script, and take the time to transfer it from a book with small print to a double-spaced page that will allow you to make notes to yourself between the lines. Here are some more tips for preparing your script so that you can perform a reading more smoothly:

- Use heavy paper that is easy to handle, and type in a font style that is easy to read, usually a serif type such as Palatino, Times New Roman, Bookman Old Style, or New Century School Book. Experiment and choose what looks best for you.
- Use only one side of the paper.
- Use a much larger font size than is normal for typing.
- Center the type on the page and keep the lines about four to five inches in length so that your eye can easily pick up the words.
- Use dots, dashes, and extra spaces instead of commas to prompt you for pauses.
- Put **key words** in **bold** type to emphasize them.
- Try using double spaces between lines of a single sentence, triple spaces between sentences, and four spaces between paragraphs.
- Keep sentences complete on a page, so that you don't have to turn the page in the middle of a thought.

• Start each main point at the top of a new page, even if you leave the preceding page three-fourths blank. You will find that every time you start a new page, you will automatically inject new energy into your voice, which is vital to getting a new point across.

• Number your pages to make sure they are in correct order, but keep them unattached so that you can slide a page over to the side as you finish. If you turn the corners up at the top or bottom before the talk, it will be easier to grab hold of the page.

As you practice reading, follow this pattern: Scan a phrase, retain, look up, and deliver. You may feel you are going too slowly, but the audience will appreciate how the pace helps them digest what you are reading. You want to make sure you are looking at your audience when you begin and end each sentence, so keep your head and voice directed up and out to the listener, not down on your script. If you tend to drop your head or read too quickly, restrict the text to the top two-thirds of the page. Choreograph and practice the movements until they feel automatic and comfortable.

If you are going to read from a text, it is helpful to use a lectern. Check it out ahead of time to see if it will accommodate your script. Find a relaxed distance from the text. (Will you need your bifocals?) Do you want the surface flat or do you need to prop it up? Will there be adequate lighting? You could bring along a book light just in case. (Remember to pack a spare bulb.) If a lectern is not appropriate or available, assemble your script in book form. Use loose-leaf or spiral binding and a firm cover, preferably in smaller format, perhaps 5 × 7, so that you can gracefully hold it in one hand while turning the pages.

And you thought having something to read would make the task easier than just speaking! It takes skill and practice to be effective. All of this preparation is essential if you are to project vitality and avoid lulling the audience to sleep with dreams of how next time they'll just ask for a copy of the text to read, rather than sitting through the droning recitation of a bedtime story.

PUT THE MULTI IN THE MEDIA

There are many good reasons to use visual aids. When chosen carefully, visual aids inject interest, strengthen organization, support the message, and create a more lasting impression. They build and maintain enthusiasm and keep the audience on its toes by varying the pace of the talk. They help visual learners understand complex relationships among your main points. They allow you to present difficult concepts in a logical sequence, stimulate your listeners' imaginations, and increase their ability to remember what you have said. Last but not least, visuals help *you* to keep focused on the key points you want to make.

Now, having sung the praises of visual aids, I must issue a warning about their overuse. Don't allow visual aids to interfere with your interaction with the audience. Use them to supplement—not substitute for—your presentation. Keep in mind that YOU are the best visual aid, because you can move around, respond to the moment, and interact with the audience. They came to hear you, not to attend a taped show.

In order for your interpretations, your energy, your passion, and your experience to command power, you must remain central to the presentation at all times. Therefore, be highly selective about any aids you choose to incorporate. A good rule of thumb is to eliminate the use of visuals for simple ideas that can be easily verbalized: "When in doubt, throw it out." It is especially important to avoid using visuals in the very beginning of a presentation when eye contact and unbroken focus is vital for establishing rapport. What follows is a summary for each of the most commonly used visual aids.

Handling Handouts

Handouts can enhance your presentation in several ways. They may include an outline of your talk, background articles, resources, or brochures. Some may serve as a structure and support for note-taking to reinforce content and help listeners follow the presentation. Handouts can be shared with others who could not attend. They also serve as a keepsake and memory jogger for later reference and networking—a key marketing tool if you are hoping for future bookings. Avoid running out of copies by checking with your contact person for an update about expected attendance, and then make extra copies just in case.

There is no one best way to distribute handouts because it all depends on how you want to use them. If they include background materials for a discussion, it is best to distribute them in advance of your talk. If you want listeners to use them as an outline, hand them out at the beginning, but know that audience members will immediately begin leafing through them. Many experts will tell you to hold off distributing handouts until the end of the talk to avoid potential distraction. Perhaps they find that postponing distribution encourages people with short attention spans to stick around until the end of the program. Personally, when I'm in the audience I feel frustrated when information is withheld. As a speaker, I prefer to trust that my listeners can recover their focus after they have a quick look, and I explain how and when we will refer to the handouts. One of the main reasons I offer handouts is to provide listeners with a systematic way to take notes. If you decide to distribute handouts at the end, try holding off on referring to them, and keep them out of sight until the appropriate moment.

Overhead Projectors

Advantages:
- It is not necessary to turn off the lights.
- You can maintain eye contact with audience.
- Transparencies are inexpensive and easy to create (on almost any printer or photocopy machine).
- Reusable.

Disadvantages:
- Bulky machine.
- Subject to breakdowns.
- Fan makes noise.
- Not appropriate for groups over 100.

Suggestions:
- Tilt the screen forward and place it in the corner at a diagonal to keep the machine from blocking the view.
- Mount the transparencies in cardboard frames; then use the edges to write notes (the new "flip frames" are good for this purpose and they organize your transparencies neatly into a binder).
- Include color graphics. A good printer can generate dazzling pictures of a quality competitive with slides.
- Overhead letters should be at least ¼" to ⅜" high.
- Never use regular copy size (font 10 to 12 is way too small).
- Write on the transparency as you are discussing, to highlight key ideas and customize to the audience needs. Watercolor markers for overheads will wipe off for reuse.
- Stand to the side, face front, and keep eye contact with the audience.
- Use a pen or pointer on the overhead, not on the screen.
- Turn the machine off when you are not focusing on an overhead.

Flip Charts

Advantages:
- Easy to prepare.
- Inexpensive.
- Semipermanent.
- Can tear off and tape up sheets to view several at a time.
- Keyed to the discussion. Generate a sense of immediacy.

Disadvantages:
- Can't erase.
- Can't use with large group.
- Continuous cost.
- Bulky to transport.

Suggestions:
- Use blank pages to keep information hidden until needed.
- Turn the page to expose a blank when you're finished referring to it.
- Tape on smaller sheets to cover part of page.
- Cut out windows or stagger lengths to create overlay effect.
- Use two or three colors; alternate each line's color to make it easier to scan.
- Print in letters 1″ to 2″ high.
- Pencil in notes; they won't be visible to the audience.
- Add a border and simple graphics; lightly predraw more complicated drawings.
- Tear off 2-inch strips of tape and stick them on the edges of the stand in advance, if you plan to post pages.
- Position yourself with the chart on your left if you are right-handed (right side if you are left-handed) to keep your body open to the audience when pointing, and to minimize turning away from the audience while writing.

Note: A flip chart is preferable to chalkboards or white-boards, which are not as easy to see or manipulate; obviously, notes taken on them can't be saved for future use.

Slides and Computer Projections

Advantages:
- Pictures can add vivid color and detail.
- Allow wide range of subject matter and treatment.

Disadvantages:
- Susceptible to breakdowns and upside-down slides.
- Keep the audience in a darkened room with little contact with the moderator.
- Create a strong temptation to let the visual presentation predominate.

Suggestions:
- Use remote control whenever possible so that you can stay mobile and face your audience.
- Insert a black slide at points where an explanation is needed, or a title slide to make a transition.
- Make duplicate copies of any slides that need to be shown more than once.
- Make the first slide a title slide. Include the names of all contributors.
- Ensure that the concluding slide leaves the audience with your message represented clearly, succinctly, vividly.

Objects, Videos, and Tape Players

If you have models, mock-ups, samples, or props that will en-hance your presentation, be sure to walk into the audience to show them briefly, and then make them available for closer scrutiny at the end of the session. Although these visuals can add great interest, you will distract your audience for a long period of time if you pass objects around during the presentation.

Playing a video during the course of your talk will appeal to the audience's orientation toward television, but this is best reserved for a longer presentation unless it is created specifically for this event. If you have only thirty minutes, and you use fifteen of them showing a video, you will deprive the audience of other information not readily available in different forms. If, however, you are planning a day-long workshop, a relevant video can be an opportunity for you to present support for your topic while giving everyone a rest from the "live" presentation.

Audiotapes can add atmosphere or background music to certain types of talks. If, however, you are using a tape to allow a speaker who is not present to offer support for your topic or another point of view, you must limit the amount of time the tape runs. It is difficult for most people to remain focused on a spoken-word tape without additional visual support. When you plan to use a tape, test it ahead of time to make sure the volume is adjusted appropriately and that it is cued to begin at the desired place when you push the play button. Check the volume in relation to the size of the room, and, if necessary, be sure there are speakers attached that will allow everyone to hear without straining.

BE CREATIVE

Developing these varied, effective visual aids is an exciting, creative part of preparing for a presentation. The best aids are simple in design, and they reflect the adage, "less is more." The goal is to reinforce your message, not show off the power of your new software or the glitz of your electronics. Yet it is essential to make each aid interesting and attractive. For simple lists, a handout is best.

Observe these guidelines in designing your aids:

• Keep them simple. Make only one main point with each visual aid. Two simple slides may be better than one complicated slide.

• Ensure that any aids you use are attractive and in good condition, with a neat and professional appearance so that they add, rather than detract, from your image.

• Title each visual.

• Present a unified, cohesive image. Use the same color scheme, font style, and size for each concept.

• Keep them uncluttered, with ample space between and around lines.

• Use key words only, not whole sentences.

• Use short words when possible.

• Aim for 5 lines, 5 words each (never more than 10 lines or 10 words) with a maximum of 36 words plus title per slide.

• Eliminate all unessential details, such as mileage scales on maps and footnotes.

• Proofread carefully. "Bee wear of spell Czech miss's."

• Avoid overly detailed tables or graphs. Use fewer than 30 numbers per visual. It's best to show only the totals.

• Make them easily visible—even from the back of the room.

• Add such graphics as borders, pictures, and cartoons. Bear in mind that the larger the symbol, the greater the impact.

• Consider using transparent overlays to create a series that gradually builds in complexity.

• Inject color to enhance interest and for ease of visual interpretation. Use two or three colors at the most to express and highlight ideas. Make use of the psychology of colors, such as our conditioned responses to red (stop), green (go), and amber (yield). Do you want your audience to react warmly or coolly to your idea or project? Warm colors include red, yellow, gold, brown, bright green, orange. Cool colors include blue, gray, light green, pastels. Primary colors convey a strong message, whereas pastels seem wishy-washy. Muddy hues imply muddy ideas. Choose colors that will be easy to read under a range of light conditions. Avoid red, blue, magenta and green type. Royal blue makes an excellent background color.

The logistics of visual aids can be very tricky. They require the care of a dedicated director and stage manager. To use them successfully, take the time to orchestrate carefully and rehearse diligently—at least twice if not three or four times. Make sure the appropriate equipment will be available and in good working order. Get the pager number of the facilities person. Be assertive with staff and hold the needs of the audience uppermost. You are not imposing by asking for whatever you need—that is the primary job of the facility.

Become familiar with any equipment. Learn where the control switches are and test them out. Have spare parts (e.g., bulbs) and extension cords available. You may need a plug adapter. Focus and test ahead of time. Organize your materials carefully. Number cards, slides, or overheads so that you can keep them in order. Consider where you will place them before and after each use. Position projectors and screens at a 45-degree angle and slightly to one side of the center of the room. This allows the presenter to occupy the central position and minimizes obstruction of view by the projector. Set the room up and check all vantage points for visibility. Go all the way to the back and extreme sides. Do posts or the chandeliers block the view? Test out easels ahead of time. (I have wrestled with many a falling flip chart.) Whenever possible, check the room out the night before. Or at least arrive an hour early.

Carefully consider how and when you will introduce your visual aids. Keep them covered and keep equipment turned off except during use. Move them out of sight once they have served their purpose. Decide in advance whether the audience should focus on you or the visual at any given point, and guide their attention accordingly. Keep your shoulders oriented and open toward the audience at a slight angle. This way you can glance over your shoulder when necessary, but you don't turn your back on your listeners. If writing on a chart keeps you from having eye contact, stop talking until you can turn back to the audience. Keep your focus on the *audience* and on your *information*, not on the aid. Resist becoming media centered. Stay people centered, and remember that rapport and interaction are much more important than any media. Finally, when you have finished your talk, end as you began—with *presence—your* presence, not the media you have used. Having turned all the equipment off and the lights back on, position yourself front and center. Reconnect strongly with your listeners and end with zest.

SMILE! YOU'RE ON CAMERA

Are you going to be videotaped, participate in a video conference, or be on TV? Remember: *Stop, Center, Breathe, Relax.* With some information and preparation, you can enjoy this opportunity.

Pay attention to what you wear. Avoid shiny or stiff material, loud patterns, excessive jewelry, and large amounts of black, white, or navy. The best colors for TV are solid pastels, beige, browns, blues, and grays. White can add pounds to your appearance. Avoid wearing red or yellow as they will bleed into the face. Makeup will help keep you from looking washed out. Keep your hair out of your eyes—preferably an inch above your eyebrows.

Select a blouse or blazer you can conveniently clip the lavaliere mike to, unless you check ahead and find out they have medallion-style mikes. Be careful not to touch the mike—and always assume it is on, so be careful what sounds and words emanate from you. Many an interviewee has been embarrassed by being caught off guard.

Remember to project your voice and speak with vitality and energy. The camera magnifies everything—including fatigue or lifelessness; hence, it tends to flatten people, making them bland and less exciting. Yet the camera also exaggerates movement since there is less background to balance motion, so eliminate any extraneous actions—no swaying in that swivel chair or tapping on the table. Smooth and slow down your gestures. I remember seeing my first TV interview on video. I was mortified to see how my active listening skills made me look like one of the bobbing-head dolls you see in back windows of cars.

Always look at the person interviewing you, not at the camera or the monitor. Don't worry about the camera's angle. There's a professional on the job! Keep direct eye contact with your interviewer. Try not to look away when thinking. If you are being taped solo or you're being interviewed by satellite with the moderator at a different site, imagine that the person you are talking to is just inside the camera lens. Visualize her smiling, friendly face to help you maintain a sense of personal interaction.

When being taped while you give a presentation or interview, check to see what is behind you. Are there distracting signs or incongruous symbols? If you are talking about recycling, you don't want to stand in front of a display of disposable diapers. Avoid places where people wander around behind you or smirk into the camera. For audio recordings or phone interviews, eliminate background noise. Turn off the radio, or you may be interrupted by horrid shrieks of feedback. Sit up—or, better, stand up—and project with dynamic enthusiasm.

Lights, camera, action. You're ready and looking good.

Remember Murphy's law? Whatever can go wrong will go wrong? The antidote is the old Boy Scout motto: Be prepared! Especially in terms of planning for the possible collapse of your plans, you must anticipate contingencies. Have a backup solution for making your presentation without the visual aids. Bring extra bulbs. Pack scissors, masking tape, and markers. Clock. Paper and pens. A small flashlight in case there is a blackout. A Swiss army knife with multiple tools "just in case." Extension cord. Plug converters. Check to see that plugs and equipment are compatible. Bring a duplicate set of notes, script, or slides. Have a master set of handouts. If anything does go awry, resist the urge to express your woe. Minimize the problem and reassure the audience that they will still get the primary message. How about cards or brochures for networking or marketing? Name tags or a sign-up sheet with markers. Pack along extra personal items: a spare pair of panty hose, safety pins, earring backings, and a water bottle. Most important, pack a flexible attitude so that you will be ready to adapt to the situation.

The techniques and tools presented in this chapter provide your twenty-first-century listeners with variety, ambience, multimodalities, and changes of pace. The key for you is to have fun using them.

MAKING THE JOURNEY

Congratulations! You've begun a lifelong journey; here are simple ways to foster continuous development and refinement of your speaking skills.

It's never too late to be what you might have been.
—GEORGE ELIOT

We have made a grand tour of speaking journeys—from impromptu to formal, from networking to dealing with the media. We visited ways to answer questions, lead discussions, persuade, inspire, and inform. Though we need to pack uniquely and plan a different mode of travel for each speaking excursion, we always orient ourselves by the same compass points: Reflect upon the listener, clarify the message and intent, and determine how to connect these within the context. Thus each journey begins by digging into our hearts and beliefs and listening to our audience.

Speaking trips become lighter and more inviting when we remember to leave worries and doubts behind and unpack myths, unlike my favorite cartoon character Cathy, who schleps all the things she should have done, ways she should have acted, and things she should have said. "Even when I'm not going anywhere," Cathy wails, "I have 300 pounds of luggage with me." We will pack lightly and remember just to be ourselves with our own style, using our nervousness as a source of dynamic energy for the jaunt.

SEEK OUT OPPORTUNITIES

You're packed and ready to go. All that may be lacking is the occasion to show your stuff. If you wait for invitations, they may not come. So how do you create opportunities? Everyday speaking abounds in presentation possibilities when you seize the chance. For example:

- Offer to review a novel you want to recommend to your book club.
- Suggest the need to promote responsible pet ownership, and volunteer to be a spokesperson at the community center.
- Read a favorite Emily Dickinson poem to your child's class, and explain how it symbolizes the seasons.
- Share your knowledge about *objets d'art* at a garage sale.

You can go beyond chance occasions and actively market yourself. When you are willing to volunteer your time, many organizations will welcome you. Call the program chair of any group that interests you. If the group has monthly meetings, you can be sure they struggle to find interesting speakers. Think of your local Chamber of Commerce, the League of Women Voters, the Junior League, a quilters association. I have often picked up flyers from groups and conferences that have programs compatible with my interests and the message I would like to send, then called the contact person to find out how to be considered for next time. They are always receptive and often grateful to learn of new resources, so I've learned it never hurts to inquire.

One friend of mine sent a letter to all the dermatologists in her area to offer to talk to them and their staffs about the dev-astating effects of alopecia (hair loss) on women and children, and to counsel them on patient needs for sensitivity and resources. Several practitioners responded and, ultimately she was invited to speak at the state association's annual conference.

Don't wait to put yourself "out there" until you feel guaranteed of results. My friend Carolyn Wildflower told me about her first venture into public speaking, which took place at a rally against nuclear weapons. She said that the words seemed to come to her from someplace outside of herself. She felt called to do it, although she had no idea what could be accomplished by her words. She was amazed to find the chain of events this talk led to, including letters from listeners who were inspired. Later she turned her remarks into magazine articles. The experience made her think of the activists who sent grains of wheat to President Eisenhower, who never realized until many years later that their actions had deeply impacted his decision not to drop nuclear bombs. You may not get results when you speak out. But you will certainly not get results when you don't. Go forth!

You can do it! Here's the experience of a friend and client, Dr. Christy Lee Engel, when she was asked to offer an invocation as "Keeper of the Community Spirit" for the Bastyr University convocation: "Although I had a clear idea of what I wanted to say, I was nervous about my ability to present it with grace and power to the audience of approximately two hundred. I called Susan in a bit of a panic! She coached me in the perspective that my presentation was a precious gift that the audience would be pleased to receive. This allowed me to deliver my invocation slowly and clearly and with enjoyment! And I received many compliments afterwards on how beautiful it was."

Engage in every conversation, no matter how large the crowd. It's still everyday one-on-one conversation, just with lots of people listening. Consider the perspective of Joan Baez: "The easiest kind of relationship for me is with ten thousand people. The hardest is with one." Check the Web page (www.toastmasters) or your phone book for Toastmasters. Volunteer for that committee you've been meaning to join. Become a board member. Join a book group. Sign on to one of the multilevel marketing products. Network. Get out there! Take some continuing education classes. Above all, resolve to contribute to every gathering.

Why not consider offering a class. I began the transition from my profession as speech therapist to training and organizational consultant by volunteering to offer workshops at the YMCA. Through trial and error in that low-key setting, I polished and honed my approach and materials.

MAKE SPEAKING AN EXPANDED CONVERSATION

No matter what the size of the occasion or of the audience, speaking is built on the relationship between you and your listeners. Think of it as an expanded conversation, and you can practice your private way of speaking, rather than feel compelled to put on a speaker's hat. When you try to convince your garden club to join together to sponsor an inner-city pea patch, the members aren't responding to you as a symbolic figure, expert, or performer, but as a real human being. When you are lively, unpredictable, and spontaneous in ways that signal your living, responsive presence, you sow interest. It's you just being yourself, not acting a role or bringing a wheelbarrow full of techniques.

You can speak effectively without remembering any special tricks. We've learned a number of effective strategies for organizing our messages, but the techniques are like luxury accommodations. The only necessities are clear thinking, a thorough understanding of the subject shaped by insight, and regard for the audience, all tied together with deep conviction and integrity. Better to have a rough outline and a fresh countenance, sizzling energy, and a sharp mind than a polished piece that's left you worn out, lifeless, and dull.

In a diverse world where audiences are varied according to culture, education, personality, and gender, translate what you know into language your listener can understand from her point of view and within her frame of reference. Just as you prepare a good meal, provide digestible information in just the right quantity, varied in texture, taste, and appearance. You don't need exotic ingredients. "If we use common words on a great occasion, they are the more striking, because they are felt at once to have a particular meaning, like old banners, or everyday clothes, hung up in a sacred place," wrote George Eliot.

TAKE THE ROAD TO RECOVERY

What happens if you slip and fall? Just get back up and take it in stride! I know it's possible. I have spilt water, knocked over flip charts, forgotten handouts, gotten lost, and arrived late. Being poised does not mean being perfect. Everyone has accidents. What matters is that you learn and grow from such experiences. Recall the wisdom of Sri Aurobindo: "By your stumbling the world is perfected." After each speaking experience, rigorously review all aspects to identify every element that went well, and analyze the critical factors that led to your success. Begin to envision how next time you will do even better. Create these learning opportunities by seeking input. You can do it informally, in writing, by phone. Just be sure to ask audience members, call the host, check with friends who attended.

When I give workshops I always solicit evaluations from participants and gain valuable insights from them. I have had to learn not to take audience reactions personally. It is almost always true that while twenty-six out of twenty-eight people may mark a session as outstanding, there will be one or two who are disappointed. I take their specific criticism seriously, but I also understand that I might have simply reminded them of their husband's ex-wives!

Know that there will be speaking attempts that fizzle for a variety of reasons. You might have a great message, but you might be giving it at the wrong time, or in the wrong place, or to the wrong people. I recall two sessions that I gave on WIN/WIN communication. The first was at a conference for women government employees. The audience was responsive, sharp and appreciative. The session was dynamite. Yet the very next week I offered a similar interactive session for the Department of Transportation with disappointing results. There were many contributing factors: The participants' morale was poor; they were obliged to be there. The room had columns and metal chairs instead of the attractive surroundings of the convention center. I worked hard to turn this discouraging day into a source of learning. I came up with some ideas to try next time that would incorporate greater insight into the very difficult challenges faced by road flaggers and project engineers. As Beverly Sills admonishes, "You may be disappointed if you fail, but you are doomed if you don't try."

An important lesson I have learned through experiencing such difficult sessions is how much worse I make it if I reveal any hint of my frustration or discouragement. If I'd rather be home, so would they. If I'm bored, grumpy, or tired, they'll see me and raise me one. Take it from me, the audience mirrors your mood. If you don't like them, they won't like you. During a break while speaking to the Department of Transportation, I remembered to fill my mind with affirmations: I belong here, I have important things to say, and people want to hear me speak. I breathed deeply and worked on opening my heart and approaching the group from their perspective. The transformation was astonishing. Where I managed to "give" in spite of my frustration, I ended up "receiving"—interest, acceptance, encouragement, even compliments.

ACTING NATURAL DOESN'T JUST COME NATURALLY: PRACTICE!

Being a good storyteller and speaker isn't just a gift of the moment. It takes practice and polish like a stand-up comedian who fine-tunes her rhythm, pace, and punch lines. Build on your strengths, and rehearse and drill yourself to enhance your talents. But at the same time, be true to yourself. Don't practice trying to imitate someone else. Study those you admire, yet find your own style.

I always admired my friend Joyce's way of capturing simple moments in life and polishing them into sparkling jewels. Over the years, I realized she tells the same story over and over, yet she knows how to judge the retelling so that I'm never bored but enjoy each recitation, like hearing a favorite poem again. With each retelling, she gains more finesse. You, too, can prepare your repertoire. Refine your funny stories of blind dates, mix-ups in time, embarrassing moments, coincidences, zany relatives, weird gifts.

So practice. Get out that video. Use your tape recorder every week and tune up your voice. Opportunities for rehearsal abound. Welcome red lights and traffic jams as opportunities to practice in the car. Linger while fixing your hair or putting on your makeup. Use those opportune, everyday moments—answering the phone, introducing yourself to a new acquaintance, or meeting your child's teacher after school—to follow the lead of MRS. P. introduced in Chapter 3, and organize your thoughts before you speak.

OUTWARD VOICE, INNER JOURNEY

"One must talk. That's how it is. One must," according to Marguerite Duras, contemporary French novelist. As a woman you have important things to say, and the world needs to hear them. Be courageous and speak with your butterflies. If you are silent and sit back comfortably, the world will miss the benefit of your experience. "How quickly does lack of speech turn into lack of identity?" asks German author Christa Wolf.

The journey begins within, and there are times when the speaking journey can take you into whole new realms of self-identity. The compass points the direction; the road map offers a path and shows what destinations are possible, with routes in and out; but only your deep belief and desire to share a message tells you which trip to take. It becomes a joyride when you put yourself into the message—when you hook yourself, as I did in writing this book. You don't have to go for glitter and glitz. You only need to refine, explore, and expose your deep attachment to whatever you are talking about, whether it's dahlias, contra dancing, or world peace. You'll be surprised to find that the benefit is even greater for yourself than for the listener. Every time you take the opportunity to speak from your deep convictions, you will learn more about yourself.

I have experienced moments when I have managed to pull out all the stops. It tends to happen when I repeat a segment of a presentation, or a poem, or a favorite passage recited often. I feel free, as though a circuit breaker has been released and all my vitality is available. I feel a rush of two-way, electrifying energy that flows from me to the audience and from the audience to me, and the feeling is purely magical. This vital life force must be what performing artists experience and generate. Between the audience and me I feel there develops a kind of community, and I remember the words of Indira

Gandhi: "Never forget that when we are silent, we are one. And when we speak, we are two."

BON VOYAGE

Please write when you venture off on your speaking treks! Share your journeys—successes and challenges, lessons learned, lessons needed. Each of the chapters in *Everyday Speaking for All Occasions* represents one of the workshops I offer, and your experiences would serve to enrich the suggestions I share with others in those sessions. Send your E-mail to <Womenspeak@aol.com> or faxes to (206) 782-7786; or write to me: Susan Partnow, 4425 Baker Ave. NW, Seattle, WA 98107.

I have worked hard to accomplish my mission in writing this book. I have tapped into my patience and discipline and dug deep to share my experience and creativity with you. May it bring you the inspiration, courage, and support you need to bring your voice to the world. Join me on the path with my mantra: "I am courageous and terrified. I dance with my fear."

Think of developing your speaking talents every day. It's a lifelong journey. Put yourself out there; reach beyond the familiar. "Security is mostly a superstition. It does not exist in nature," wrote Helen Keller. "Life is either a daring adventure or nothing at all." Good luck and bon voyage!

Resources

The number of books, articles, and resources available for speakers is mind boggling. Hundreds are published each year. There are self-help books; anthologies of jokes, quips and speeches; tapes, videos, and, of course, specialty resources for every area of interest. I am often inspired by my favorite cartoons: "The Far Side," "For Better or Worse," "Sally Forth," "Dilbert," "Ashleigh Brilliant." Check out your library, bookstore, or book dealer, and you are certain to find resources that will suit you. Below are just a few suggestions:

Bianchi, Sue, Jan Butler, and David Richey. *Warmups for Meeting Leaders.* University Associates, 1990.
Felton, Bruce, and Mark Fowler. *The Best, Worst & Most Unusual.* Galahad Books, 1994.
Jones, Judy, and William Wilson. *An Incomplete Education.* Ballantine Books, 1995.
Partnow, Elaine T. *The New Quotable Woman.* Facts on File, 1992.
Wallechinsky, David, and Irving Wallace. *The People's Almanac* and *The Book of Lists.* Numerous editions.

TAPES:

Many of the books on speaking exist as audiocassettes as well as books. Many are available through your library. Here are a few suggestions:

Never Be Nervous Again, Dorothy Sarnoff, 1992.
The Power of Your Voice, Carol Fleming, Ph.D., 1989.

Smart Speaking: 60 Second Strategies for Speaking Problems & Fears,
   Laurie Schloff and Marcia Yudkin, 1993.
Look for *The Speaker's Voice* by David Stern.

I recommend listening to recordings of great literature and poems
read by actors with inspiring voices. Relaxation and confidence-boosting
tapes are also useful. I like those by Dr. Emmett Miller, including *Healing Journey* and *Letting Go of Stress*. Also look for *The Fine Art of Relaxation* by Joel Levy, *Stress Reduction and Creative Meditations* by
Marc Allen, and *What I Believe/Deep Relaxation* by Louise Hay. Go to
a store where they will let you listen before you make your purchase to
ensure that you are soothed and not irritated by the speaker's voice.

Toastmasters has prepared an affordable video, *Be Prepared to Speak,*
by Kantola Skeie Productions. Check the reference section of your favorite video store and the library for others as well.

A FEW FAVORITE BOOKS:

Ailes, Roger, with Jon Kraushar. *You Are the Message: Secrets of the Master Communicators.* Dow Jones–Irwin, 1988.
Boettinger, Henry M. *Moving Mountains, or the Art of Letting Others See Things Your Way.* Collier Books, MacMillan, 1969.
Bolton, Robert. *People Skills: How to Assert Yourself, Listen to Others, and Resolve Conflicts.* Touchstone, Simon & Schuster, 1979.
Frank, Milo. *How to Get Your Point Across in 30 Seconds or Less.* Harper & Row, 1991.
Gabor, Don. *Talking with Confidence for the Painfully Shy.* Crown, 1997.
Hamlin, Sonya. *How to Talk So People Listen: The Real Key to Job Success.* Harper & Row, 1988.
Hoff, Ron. *I Can See You Naked,* rev. Andrews & McMeel, 1992. (a guide to fearless presentations)
Josefowitz, Natasha. *Paths to Power: A Woman's Guide from First Job to Top Executive.* Addison-Wesley Publishing Company, 1980.
Kahn, Michael. *The Tao of Conversation.* New Harbinger, 1995.
Kroeger, Otto, and Janet M. Thuesen. *Type Talk: The 16 Personality Types That Determine How We Live, Love and Work.* Delta, 1988.
Lakoff, Robin Tolmach. *Talking Power: The Politics of Language.* Basic Books, Harper Collins, 1990.

LeVasseur, Robert E. *Breakthrough Business Meetings.* Bob Adams, 1994.

Marsheel, Jeannie. *Energetic Meetings: Enhancing Personal and Group Energy and Handling Difficult Behaviors.* Jemel Publishing House, 1994.

Mayer, Lyle. V. *Fundamentals of Voice & Diction,* 7th ed. Wm. Brown, 1985. (comprehensive with many exercises)

Ristad, Eloise. *A Soprano on Her Head.* Real People Press, 1982. (performance anxiety)

Stone, Janet, and Jane Bachner. *Speaking Up: A Book for Every Woman Who Talks.* Carroll & Graf, 1994.

Tannen, Deborah. *You Just Don't Understand: Women and Men in Conversation.* William Morrow Co., 1990.

Viles, Donna. *Power Networking.* Mt. Harbour Publications, 1992.

Wilder, Claudyne. *The Presentations Kit,* rev. John Wiley & Sons, 1994.

Woodwall, Marian K. *Thinking on Your Feet.* Warner Books, 1996.

RESOURCES ON THE INTERNET:

Dive in and try surfing the Net! It gets easier, more enjoyable, and mind-boggling every moment. Women! We must partake of this new medium and make our voices heard, loud and clear. Indeed, it's a perfect match for our collaborative style. E-mail provides vital glue in creating community and sustaining relationships.

There are many resources for speakers on the Internet. I like to use a variety of Web search engines, found at <http://home.netinc.ca/%7Ed-sardo/search.html>, although my current best successes tend to come with Alta Vista (http://www.altavista.digital.com/). For example, I found these lovely toasts while surfing one day:

Mothers hold their children's hands for just a little while . . .
And their hearts forever.

May I see you gray
And combing your grandchildren's hair.

You can find a treasure chest of resources for quotations. I found one Web site devoted to quotation links (http://www.starlingtech.com/quotes/links.html), which led me to many great collections, including

<http://www.trg2.saic.com/~jeff/sw/quotations.html>. I found the following among great women's quotations when directed to this Web page at <www.lexmark.com/data/quote.html>:

Ingrid Bergman: "I have no regrets. I wouldn't have lived my life the way I did if I was going to worry about what people were going to say."

Harriet Braiker: "Striving for excellence motivates you; striving for perfection is demoralizing."

Dame Margot Fonteyn: "Take your work seriously, but never yourself."

Margaret Fuller: "If you have knowledge, let others light their candles in it."

At the Web page for Toastmasters (www.toastmasters) I was referred to some interesting shareware called *The Speaker's Companion—About Your Personal Public Speaking Coach* (http://www.lm.com/%7Echipp/spkrcmpn.htm)

There is an extensive collection of facilitators' resources and information, which you can link to from an excellent Web page (http://www.oise.on.ca/~bwillard/facinfo.html). I have also found some interesting women's pages, including *Beatrice's Web Guide* (http://www.bguide.com/), which led me to *Gender-Free Pronoun Frequently Asked Questions* (http://www.eecis.udel.edu/%7Echao/gfp/#issues) and *Empowering Women in Business* (http://www.feminist.org/research/ewb_myths.html).

And, of course, whatever your content or subject interest, vast global resources are just a click away!